A Picture of the
Peak District

overleaf: *Hollinsclough hamlet*

A Picture of the Peak District

ROGER A. REDFERN

Illustrated by
GORDON PARKIN

ISBN 0 7090 2965 9

Robert Hale Limited
Clerkenwell House
Clerkenwell Green
London EC1R 0HT

British Library Cataloguing in Publication Data
Redfern, Roger A.
   A picture of the Peak District.
   1. Peak District National Park (England)
   —— Guide-books
   I. Title
   914.25′ 1104858   DA670.D43

Photoset in Baskerville by
Rowland Phototypesetting Limited, Bury St Edmunds, Suffolk
Printed in Great Britain by
St Edmundsbury Press Limited, Bury St Edmunds, Suffolk
and bound by WBC Bookbinders

Contents

List of Illustrations		7
Introduction		11
1	Gritstone Country of the East	15
2	True Grit – Landscape with Sheep	29
3	Villages along the Line	47
4	Highest City's Leafy Edge	55
5	Black Holes, White Rock	65
6	Rocking Stones and Standing Stones	72
7	Life on the Limestone Fringe	83
8	Townscapes	91
9	Three Rivers' Journey	109
10	Sunbeams on the Cheshire Plain	127
11	Cotton grass and Curlews	153
12	Forgotten Hill Farms	163
13	A Peakland Year	177
Bibliography		217
Index		219

List of Illustrations

Hollinsclough hamlet	*frontispiece*
Bradfield Dale from Cliffe House Farm	10
Boot's Folly overlooking the head of Bradfield Dale	14
Watch-house at the gates of Bradfield parish church	17
Yew Tree Farm, near Bolsterstone, looking to Broomhead Moor	22–3
Leash Fen and Big Moor from Clod Hall Lane	26
Yorkshire Bridge	28
Hazelford Hall looking across the Derwent valley to Bamford Edge	30–1
Fairest Clough Farm ruins, Bretton Clough	36–7
Howden Reservoir from above Gores Farm	42–3
Hathersage Church from the Dale	48
Padley Chapel, near Grindleford	49
Millstones at Lawrence Field, above Padley	51
Converted barns, Nether Shatton	53
Ecgbert Stone on Dore village green	56
Dore Moor House	58
Thomas Boulsover memorial beside Wire Mill Dam, Mayfield Valley	63
Magpie Mine, Sheldon	64
Eldon Hole	67
Eldon Hill Quarry from Rushup Edge	69
Magpie Mine	71
Stone circle on Harthill Moor	72
Rowtor Rocks, Birchover	75
Robin Hood's Stride and Cratcliffe Tor	78–9
Saxon cross, All Saints Church, Bradbourne	82
Hopton Hall	88
Kniveton village	90
Ashbourne, Church of St Oswald	92

Buxton. The Crescent from St Anne's Cliff with the Old
    Hall Hotel, the dome of the Devonshire
    Hospital and the Palace Hotel   96–7
Railway viaduct, Chapel Milton   99
Cottages, Old Glossop   100
Penistone railway viaduct and parish church from the
    north-east   105
Hollinsclough hamlet in the Upper Dove Valley   111
Upper Manifold Valley with Chrome Hill   113
Manifold Valley with Thor's Cave   120–1
Throwley Hall   124
The Torrs, New Mills   128
Chapel steps, Flash   129
Goldsitch Moss   130–1
Wincle Grange   132
Telecom Mast on Croker Hill   134
Cottages at Langley, near Macclesfield   138–9
Shrigley Hall   142
Ford Hall, near Chapel-en-le-Frith   145
The River Goyt in the Torrs, New Mills   147
Old Mills in the Torrs, New Mills looking towards
    Lyme Park   149
Head of the Chew Valley   152
Memorial to James Platt looking over Dovestone Edge   155
The old Flouch Inn, near Langsett   161
Rowlee Farm, Woodlands Valley   165
The remains of Swinden Farm above the Porter Valley,
    near Langsett   168
Cruck barn interior   171
Hallfield overlooks the head of Bradfield Dale   172–3
Sunset from behind Stanage Edge   178–9
Windgather Rocks near Kettleshulme   185
Deer in the snow at Chatsworth   190–1
Manifold Valley   196
Alsop-en-le-Dale   202
Ramshaw Rocks from Morridge   207
Rocking stones, Crow Stones Edge, Howden Moors   212–13
The western portal of Totley Tunnel at Padley, near
    Grindleford   214
General map   13

Bradfield Dale from Cliffe House Farm

Introduction

The Peak District is almost surrounded by densely populated lowlands. For that reason it is one of the most popular upland districts of Britain; a favourite on account of its proximity to so many folk and because its three major rock types create a contrast in landscapes within a comparatively small compass.

The Carboniferous limestone is the oldest of these rocks, outcropping to form an area of white-walled pastoral country and deep, sometimes dry valleys. The brown millstone grit gives wilder, higher terrain – edges and plateaux and old farms which melt into their sheltering hillsides. The coal measures border the eastern fringe of Peakland, eroded by weathering into verdant, hill-and-valley country.

There are many pressures on the district. This century has seen the intensification of limestone quarrying in the White Peak, the construction of great reservoirs for Midlands' water supply, and adjacent coniferous plantings.

Many books have appeared through the years describing various facets of this fairly compact piece of England but I have endeavoured here to sum up recent changes and to put the present character of the area in perspective. The Peak District National Park has an area of 542 square miles but I have not confined myself to this boundary for there is a lot of wonderful country beyond the Park boundary.

As Patrick Monkhouse wrote in the sixties, the Peak District is more than a landscape: it's a landscape with figures. It has a larger human population than other National Parks, and here a war is constantly being waged – people versus places, a battle to prevent the insidious, gnawing advances of urban man and his schemes, be they an inappropriate alteration to a cottage or extension of a quarry face. The National Park authority, based at Bakewell, has done much enlightened conservation work and planning control through the years, though we may not approve of some of its popularization policies which result in removal of that feeling of personal discovery of countryside, of coming unexpectedly on an unselfconscious corner. Information boards and signposted picnic sites are not synonymous with true exploration.

There is no doubt that the best way to discover the real secrets of any landscape is on foot. Much of this text is based on my own pedestrian wanderings; many will, doubtless, follow and enjoy the flavour of hidden country, see grouse curving in low flight near the head of the Derwent, and grey squirrels scamper in the beeches at Broomhead, and hear curlews calling under blue June skies on Holme Moss.

My thanks go to Mrs Winifred Craig for help with preparation of the manuscript, including the index.

WEST YORKSHIRE

SOUTH YORKSHIRE

Penistone

River Don

GREATER MANCHESTER

Saddleworth

BLACK HILL

Chew Brook

River Tame

Glossop

Longdendale

KINDER SCOUT

BLEAKLOW

Derwent Dale

Ewden Valley

Bradfield

Bradfield Dale

Sheffield

Hayfield

New Mills

Edale

Hope

Castleton

Bamford

EASTERN

Lyme Park & Hall

Chapel-en-le-Frith

Hathersage

Pott Shrigley

CHESHIRE

DERBYSHIRE

EDGES

Dronfield

Langley

Buxton

River Wye

Baslow

Sutton Lane End

SUTTON COMMON

Bakewell

Chesterfield

Flash

Hollinsclough

River Dove

River Dane

Longnor

River Manifold

Stanton in Peak

Darley Dale

Birchover

Matlock

STAFFORDSHIRE MOORLANDS

Elkstone

Hartington

Matlock Bath

Leek

Butterton

Alsop-en-le-Dale

Onecote

Grindon

Parwich

Brassington

Hopton

Wirksworth

River Derwent

STAFFORDSHIRE

River Hamps

Bradbourne

Kniveton

Hognaston

Ashbourne

0 1 2 3 4 5   10 Miles

0   5   10   15 Kilometres

National Park Boundary

County Boundaries

Rivers

▲ Summits

● Places of interest mentioned in test

Crown Copyright Reserved – The Peak District

Boot's Folly overlooking the head of Bradfield Dale

1

Gritstone Country of the East

Imagine a sharp June evening with the slanting sunlight sending long shadows across a rutted heather moor. Dunlins pipe from some far hillock, and grouse grumble to each other under the widest of upland skies.

If you move to the edge of this moorland, to the eastern fringe where it slips off towards lower ground, you gaze into a chequer-board valley looking for all the world like Swaledale. It has a certain northern Pennine magic, not typical of what we have come to associate with the Peak District. Hayfields are juxtaposed with dark pastures where cows settle for the short night. We can almost feel the dew falling on those juicy fields, wrapped around by broad hedgerows and little woods.

No major valley of the Peak District is less known by the general public than Bradfield Dale, north-west of Sheffield and lying entirely in South Yorkshire. The reason is not hard to find, though, for this broad and beautiful trough in the hills is somewhat remote. To its west rise the high gritstone moors which form Derwent Edge, separating Bradfield Dale from the popular Derwent Dale with its string of three reservoirs. The visitors who know the valley best are Sheffield folk, for its river is the Loxley which flows directly out of the countryside into the city's north-western suburbs at Malin Bridge.

To reach Bradfield Dale from the well-trodden tourist tracks of Peakland you must take the narrow hill road branching from the Sheffield–Manchester trunk road (A57) at Moscar. Quite soon there are wonderful views into the head of the dale below Strines. This latter consists of an inn which originated as a manor built in 1275 and said to this day to be haunted by a grey lady. It is a tiny settlement which retains the feel of antiquity, sheltered by aged trees at the edge of the high moors; poultry still scratch at the roadside, and straw litters the farmyard. The unusual name of the place is said to be derived from the 'strides' or stepping-stones once used to cross the stream below the inn.

That broad view into the head of Bradfield Dale from the Strines hill road reveals an imposing stone tower on the grassy slopes above Strines Reservoir, uppermost of the valley's four dams. For all its apparent antiquity, this fifty-foot-high tower dates only from 1927, when Charles Boot of the adjacent Bents House used stone and mullioned windows from demolished properties to form what is simply a folly. A wooden staircase wound up inside to the viewing platform but a cow once climbed it, got hopelessly stuck and was only rescued after considerable effort. Since that time the lower section of the staircase has been removed so that 'Boot's Folly' can no longer be used as a belvedere.

Large areas of the western slopes of upper Bradfield Dale have been planted with conifers, and these help to deflect gales blowing off the exposed Howden Moors beyond. Overlooking the western side of the second dam – Dale Dike Reservoir – is the fine seventeenth-century Hallfield, an elegant gritstone house with a very old cruck barn and until recent years part of the Fitzwilliam estates.

Little is known of Hallfield's history but much more is certain about the notorious Dale Dike Reservoir which fills the valley floor below it. Constructed in 1863–4 to satisfy the rapidly increasing demands of Sheffield, it was the first in this dale. The impounding wall was 1,200 feet long and a hundred feet high, holding 700 million cubic feet of water. It was filled quickly to satisfy the urgent needs of the city.

On 11 March 1864, 'A heavy rainfall filled the dam rapidly and a high wind, blowing down the gorge, hurled the water against the embankment in heavy waves.' A horizontal crack appeared in the wall later that day and the engineer was sent for. He did not arrive until after dark, to find a widening crack. Immediately gun-powder was placed against the overflow weir to release some of the water. The first effort failed and before anything more could be done the centre of the dam broke, liberating a thunderous deluge down the valley. Word had already spread in the villages near the valley floor, so the roar of the flood sent the inhabitants fleeing up the hillsides and out of danger. An infant washed out of its mother's arms and a labourer who had scoffed at the danger and gone to bed were the only victims in the upper dale.

Lower down, though, the flood was disastrous because people had not been alerted and the cascading waters carried large quantities of wreckage which 'thundered against doors and walls like a battering ram'. Within half an hour the flood had passed, leaving a scene described later as one of 'death and wreckage and desolation unparalleled in the annals of English towns'. A total of 4,511 houses were flooded, 39 of them totally destroyed, and 240 persons were killed. The water company had eventually to pay out £276,918 for personal injury, loss of life and damage to property and trade. The dam was reconstructed with a new wall 400 yards upsteam of the original one, work being finally completed in 1875. In the meantime Bradfield Dale had acquired three other reservoirs, and there is no obvious sign of the collapsed wall now because plantations clothe both sides of the valley.

A mile below this dam stands Low Bradfield. There are really two Bradfield settlements and this one occupies the valley floor. There is a cricket field by the little river, and attractive stone cottages and farm buildings line the lane which begins the steep climb to Bradfield, the upper settlement. The situation is magnificent. Bradfield is first mentioned as a village in 1188, and the parish church of St Nicholas was thought by J. Hunter in his *History of Hallamshire* to date from not later than the reign of Henry II (1154–89). It is certainly one of the biggest churches in the part

Watch-house at the gates of Bradfield parish church

of South Yorkshire called Hallamshire ('a shire within a shire') and is remarkable for the amount of embattlement. The west tower is probably fourteenth-century, and a lot more seems a century later.

The view from the graveyard in clear weather is wonderful, of a broad dale-head and heaped-up woods and a patchwork of fields belonging to a hundred pastoral farms. At the graveyard gates stands the unusual watch-house of 1745. When it was built, body-snatching was common, so the families of the recently deceased took nightly shelter in this building, until bacteria and earthworms had done their work and rendered the corpse useless for research. Very few watch-houses remain in Britain.

Immediately to the north-west of the graveyard stands the fifty-eight-foot-high mound known as Bailey Hill. Now tree-covered, it must have formed a formidable defensive site with its wide fosse (moat) when erected by the Normans to control this wild, remote area. At the eastern end of the village stands another earthwork, Castle Hill, where a small tower may have stood. Both sites, of course, offered broad views of the dale but the relative proximity of Sheffield Castle seven miles down the valley seems to have led to their early demise. A pre-war guidebook claimed that, 'No English city could produce a finer scene within four miles of a suburban tram terminus.'

Not far from Bailey Hill is the long exposure of gritstone cliff, half hidden by shaggy oak wood, known as Agden Rocher. The word 'rocher' is an old term for 'rock face'. It marks here the line of an old landslip of uncertain age, and in a field below it in 1888 a local archaeologist found round and horseshoe scrapers and trimmed flint flakes dating from neolithic or Early Bronze Age times. They were fashioned from what is thought to be horse bone. What a nice thought: the earliest residents working here in wind and rain, viewing the same dale but then dense-packed with woodland and the moors above probably wooded, too.

Returning to more recent times, it is surprising that Agden Rocher did not become popular with rock-climbers earlier than was the case. The late Eric Byne discovered the outcrop in the early fifties, and now it is criss-crossed with climbing routes. It is one of the most attractive gritstone crags in Peakland set as it is high above Agden Clough, with broad views to the upper dale and the heather moors beyond. It catches a good share of sunshine, too.

Near the foot of Agden Rocher stands antique Bowsen Barn, only remnant of Bowsen Farm. The house was pushed down by the old Sheffield Water Authority years ago (in line with an unenlightened policy of sweeping away as many lovely old places in their catchment area as possible), and only a pile of stones and fallen oak beams bear witness to its existence. The barn is one of a handful of magnificent cruck barns remaining in this corner of England, buildings whose exact age is unknown but around which much controversy has swung for years. It is, I think, true to call them at least medieval in origin. The stone walls and stone-slated roofs are probably replacements for former wood and thatch. The lovely, arching timbers, though, are original. Bowsen Barn is now, after years of neglect, to be used as an outdoor base for the handicapped.

One of the great attractions of Bradfield Dale is the intricate network of narrow lanes which connect the half-hidden hamlets, farms and cottages. They are bounded by a mixture of gritstone walls and hedges, depending on site and altitude. Walk the sinuous lane by Walker House and Annet Bridge to Low Bradfield in high summer and marvel at the scent and sight of honeysuckle twining the walls, and the later, heady aroma of meadowsweet in the laneside ditches near Agden Reservoir.

One of the lanes that lead eastwards towards the Don Valley, climbing to 1,135 feet from Bradfield village, later passes the gaunt, grey walls of Kirk Edge Convent of the Carmelite Order. In 1870 the barren acres of Onesmoor here were taken over for use by an orphanage, and many local folk must have chuckled at the vain attempts to cultivate the wind-swept land and cover the cost (£2,300) of the thc 189 acre site. It failed but the convent was later established on this open and forbidding hilltop, protected by a few wind-bent conifers. The Carmelite nuns came here in 1911. They claim Elijah as the first member of their order and to this day observe the strictest rules, shut away from the world by that high, stone wall. The handful of sisters live here in virtual silence, in comfortless, blank-walled rooms, and never go outside again. I wonder if they can see those broadest of views that surround Kirk Edge; can they, I wonder as I pass by, see over that gaunt wall and pick out Ferrybridge and Drax power stations far to the north-east, and York Minster and the blue line of the Yorkshire Wolds? Surely they must sometimes peep across to the hanging woods on Wharncliffe Side and, on summer evenings, admire the pink-tinged cumulus clouds in the eastern heavens.

Several footpaths traverse the slope below Kirk Edge, between Holdworth hamlet and Bradfield. The path above Holdworth Hall brings one soon to Cliffe House Farm, built in 1866, and beyond this it was formerly paved and called locally 'T'Owd Lane'. The sudden view of upper Bradfield Dale from Cliffe House Farm has been called 'the choicest surprise view of dale and moor within six miles of any large industrial city' and without equal in the Peak District. In bright weather, in any season, the green dale rising to the shadowed gritstone moors beyond takes a good deal of beating.

The next dale to the north of Bradfield is likewise beautiful, and missed by the mass of visitors. I'm sure that's a good thing and suppose it's really rather silly of me to broadcast the virtues of these peach-blossom districts of fond memory. Their remaining charm is threatened by popularity.

This next depression is the Ewden Valley, which I once described as South Yorkshire's loveliest dale. It certainly takes some beating. Its lower reaches contain two reservoirs for Sheffield – More Hall and Broomhead; its upper half is wild and untrodden and open to the breezy heights. Ewden, like Bradfield, has a maze of steep and narrow lanes, farms and cottages in warm brown stone, hanging woods and grand vistas at every turn.

Ewden village is a funny sort of spot. Originally a semi-permanent settlement when the dams were being built, it has metamorphosed into a little estate of ugly houses quite out of place near the head of More Hall Reservoir. The hill road up from the Don Valley near Wharncliffe Side to Bolsterstone passes the back of delightful, well-preserved More Hall – a real mansion – but then passes one or two hideous modern constructions obviously erected by folk with lots more money than good taste.

Bolsterstone is a lovely, hill-top village of great antiquity, famous for its choir, and almost a thousand feet above sea-level. Stocksbridge, straggling steel town of the Little Don Valley, has climbed the slopes towards the village on the northern side but does not really impinge on the rurality – yet!

A complex of tumbled, hillocky ground high on the dale's southern slope is called Canyard Hills, a mysterious name, but an earlier name for these once-timbered bumps and trenches was Mouldy Cliff, a term used elsewhere in the south Pennines to describe landslip features.

The narrow road which leaves the Sheffield–Manchester trunk road (A57) at Moscar and runs north to the other Sheffield –Manchester road (A616) at Langsett is, in my opinion, the finest upland road in all Peakland. It swerves into and out of each upper dale that it crosses – Strines, Agden and Ewden in turn – and gives a good impression of the broad, relatively smooth nature of the heather moors to the west. In July the bilberry-pickers come in force to the fringe of Broomhead Moors and the Canyard Hills; in August hundreds of acres become an emperor's carpet.

Of all the cloughs known to me ('clough' comes from the old English *cloh*, a deep ravine or a dell), Ewden's upper dale, west of the lovely hill road, is the most overgrown in summer and the most rewarding to explore. Rhododendron and bracken crowd in on a grand scale to make progress difficult. I recommend the path from near the site of Broomhead Hall, demolished a few years ago, which crosses delightful heather moor to the prehistoric stone circle only rediscovered after a recent moor fire had removed the covering vegetation. Suddenly the path goes down through trees to the dank dale-bottom. Water trickles from springs and you can totter across a footbridge of narrow railway rails without any hand support and climb up through tormenting bracken – the highest I know – to the open hill pastures at derelict Holt Farm. On a sticky late summer's day the congregation of midges adds to the challenge of this unforgettable dale.

Bilberries are not the only late-summer fare offered by these moors. Cowberry or red whortleberry grows over a wide area, in association with heather. Its hard, red berries can be picked more quickly than bilberries and make good jelly. On a gloriously hot, still August day not so long ago, I remember coming with a friend down the upper Agden clough from Derwent. The moor seemed on fire with cowberries, so I decided to pick some and set to work; my friend, though, couldn't find any, and this mystified me – until I remembered he was red-green colour-blind!

These north-eastern uplands have been less affected by change than some parts of Peakland. That is a refreshing thing, though the sight of many derelict farms is regrettable and must represent a change, albeit not too obvious at first glance across this land-scape. Is a forlorn and broken-windowed farmhouse high in a remote valley less attractive than a brashly smartened house with lashings of white paint and a row of cars on the new drive where once moor sheep wandered?

Anyone who has travelled south-westwards from Sheffield towards Baslow and the Derwent Valley, or Bakewell or Matlock, will have used the A621 road and been impressed by the wide, open spaces it traverses. The route climbs to a thousand feet at Owler Bar, then crosses high moorland country with broad vistas under great skies. This is part of the so-called Eastern Moors, an area of some 6,400 acres extending from Totley Moor in the north to the old road between Chesterfield and Baslow in the south, and

Yew Tree Farm, near Bolsterstone, looking to Broomhead Moor

westwards from Ramsley Moor to the famous gritstone edges of Froggatt and Curbar. Much of it lies above a thousand feet, and it reaches 1,300 feet on Totley Moor, near the Derbyshire–South Yorkshire boundary.

By 1982 the Severn–Trent Water Authority, owner of this wild upland, no longer needed the area for water catchment. For a hundred years the Eastern Moors had been protected from drastic change by this requirement, but now the fear was abroad that it might be threatened with agricultural improvement and commercial afforestation. The Peak Park Planning Board moved swiftly and decided that the best way to protect the area was to purchase it. If it came into private ownership, protection under the Wildlife and Countryside Act would need to be by voluntary agreement with, as the Board explained, a potential cost in annual compensation payments that in the course of a twenty-year agreement would cover the cost of acquisition several times over.

Arrangements for transfer of ownership went ahead, but in March 1983 the Peak Park Planning Board was informed by the Department of the Environment that the agreed price of £525,000 fell too far short of the valuation of £750,000 to be acceptable. Another argument was that certain tenant farmers were anxious to buy parts of the land they were farming. Eventually, however, early in 1984 the purchase price was agreed at £665,000.

What of the Eastern Moors, their character and their value? What features have lain largely undiscovered to the general public? The high and inhospitable gritstone uplands were less attractive to the ancients than the limestone plateau to the west, so it was not until the Middle Bronze Age that the former were colonized. Ramsley Moor has three stone circles and many barrows; twenty years ago no fewer than sixty-seven barrows were identified at one location. In the long drought of 1959 a fire destroyed a large area of heather on Totley Moor to reveal an earth bank enclosing a flat area containing a central cairn. Thereafter Dr J. Radley did a detailed excavation of the site and found the remains of five cremations and pottery of the Middle Bronze Age.

Intervening between the growing market towns of eastern Derbyshire and southern Yorkshire on one side and the Derwent Valley on the other, these gritstone heights developed an extensive network of packways. It is still easy to imagine packhorse trains wending their way with loads of Cheshire salt and Peak District lead towards the busy trading centre of Chesterfield.

Tangible reminders of these medieval trackways are the lonely slab bridge over the Bar Brook, not a hundred yards from the busy A621, and the several stone guide-posts on the breezy moors. Lady Cross stands on Big Moor where the Hope–Chesterfield and Sheffield–Tideswell routes crossed.

Another lonely sentinel is Godfrey's Cross on Ramsley Moor, adjacent to Fox Lane, which climbs out of the beautiful Cordwell Valley. Probably erected by the monks of Beauchief Abbey, it is lettered 'Here lies Godfrey' but this does not mark the grave of an old-time traveller: the carving was done by young Godfrey Silcock of Fox Lane before he emigrated to New Zealand about 1893. A few hundred yards away, now hidden from view by the wind-blasted conifers of Shillito Plantation, stands a taller, finer cross which may have been removed from its original site near the moor-top road junction.

The packhorse tracks and their associated guide-posts were superseded by the turnpike roads constructed between about 1750 and 1780. These more directly linked Chesterfield and Sheffield with crossing-points of the River Derwent to the west. One such is the perfectly straight Chesterfield–Curbar road created by an Act of 1745. It cuts across the moor close to Clod Hall, so named from the rough dwelling of a squatter called William Kay whose claim had not been staked long enough to be a legal right in the Baslow Enclosure Act of 1823. Three miles to the north-west of Clod Hall the road reaches 1,010 feet and passes through the shallow col called Curbar Gap, where the Derwent Valley is suddenly revealed below. Here is the dramatic north-south line of gritstone edges – Baslow, Curbar and Froggatt – which are the popular practice ground of many cragsmen.

The dukes of Rutland owned a large part of these moorlands and kept them sacrosanct. When they became important water-gathering grounds for urban areas to the east, the local water authority maintained this privacy. However, before the First World War the great pioneer rambler G. H. B. Ward was waging a battle for access to the path running along the crest of these edges. He claimed it to be 'the best of its kind in Derbyshire', giving 'a charming illustration of the panoramic changes which a short walk at an effective height may bring'. An arrangement was made that allowed parties of not more than six people to walk on these edge-tops outside the shooting and breeding seasons. This arrangement was terminated in 1924, and Ward called it 'a blot upon public ownership'.

Only after the Second World War did the water authority allow access to these grand edges, and the Valkyrie Mountaineering Club explored Froggatt and Curbar Edges during 1948 and 1949, when most of the well-known routes were pioneered by Joe Brown, Nat Allen and others. Even so, the Sheffield area climbing guide of 1951 gave the address of the North-East Derbyshire Joint Water Committee for those seeking a permit to climb here. In recent years there has been a proper access agreement between the water authority and the Peak Park Planning Board, and crowds of climbers, walkers and casual pedestrians visit this bold escarpment country every weekend and holiday.

The most remarkable part of the Eastern Moors lies at the south-eastern corner; it is the fairly level expanse of Leash Fen at an average altitude of 930 feet. An old rhyme states:

> When Leech-field was a market town,
> Chesterfield was gorse and broom.
> Now Chesterfield's a market town,
> Leech-field a marsh is grown.

By 1503 the area must have looked very much as it does today because a document of that date refers to 'Lechemeyre' – an Old English term for 'a boggy marsh'. Drainmakers working here earlier this century found the remains of oak trees, supporting the

Leash Fen and Big Moor from Clod Hall Lane

theory that impervious shales on the gritstone plateau stopped proper drainage long ago. Leash Fen is a wet area, with its tussocky margins developing to rush and sphagnum moss towards the centre. Silver birch is colonizing the drier fringes but it will be a long time before oak woodland is regenerated because of the unsuitable soil conditions.

Three miles north of Leash Fen lies Flask Edge on Totley Moor, and this gives a remarkable vista north-eastwards across Sheffield, a view which reveals just how close that fortunate city is to the high country of the Peak District. The Peak Park Planning Board says these Eastern Moors are 'of national heritage value, and their protection, enhancement and enjoyment by the public are best assured by Board ownership and management'. It is to be hoped that this management plan does not include the widespread use of car-parks, pokerwork signposts, information boards and picnic sites, which have brought an inordinate number of visitors to some parts of Peakland and destroyed those very qualities of remoteness which the Board is supposed to be protecting. The Eastern Moors should be left to go on much as before, to be discovered and wandered over by those prepared to leave the muddy track and to research the past from books at home. That is the approach that G. H. B. Ward would surely have approved.

And that great rambler would surely have chuckled at the two little boys who peered over a gap in a tumbled wall at Low Bradfield recently as I walked by. They were six years old, and one of them, a curly goldie-locks, had a stout Maran cockerel under his arm.

'Hello,' said the young poultry farmer. We had a conversation about his farm and he explained: 'I still go to school so my father looks after the place while I'm away.' I admired the speckled cockerel.

'Yes, but he doesn't lay eggs,' came the reply.

Yorkshire Bridge

2

True Grit – Landscape with Sheep

Most of the gritstone uplands of the Peak District lie to the east of the River Derwent and north of the River Noe. An exception is the outlier of the Abney, Offerton and Eyam Moors, isolated to the west of the Derwent and cut into by the deep dale called Bretton Clough.

Bretton Brook rises at almost 1,250 feet under Hucklow Edge and flows north-eastwards for four miles to join the Derwent near Leadmill Bridge, Hathersage. Halfway down the clough its name changes to become 'Highlow Brook'. Down in this wooded, road-less dale are the remnants of cottages and farms, last survivors of a busy rural world that has gone forever from this part of Peakland.

The best way to explore Bretton Clough is to set out from the Plough Inn, above Leadmill Bridge spanning the Derwent near Hathersage, and follow the ancient lane to Broadhay Farm. A footpath continues right up the dale, by Stoke Ford to Bretton village and Great Hucklow, high at the edge of the limestone plateau. On the hillside opposite Broadhay Farm, across the mouth of the Clough, stands Hazelford Hall, a delightful seventeenth-century house adorned with a typical Derbyshire porch of the period, gables with ball finials and a variety of four- and five-light mullioned windows. Its elevated position above the valley lends credence to the tradition that this was one of the Seven Hathersage Halls built by a powerful Eyre, seven halls built within sight of each other for each of his seven sons.

The lower clough is well wooded, with tasteful plantings of larch on the southern slopes above the brook. On the northern side is a dense forest of immature pine, spruce and larch that forms an attractive tapestry when seen from a second path that traverses the southern slope. Highlow Hall (another traditional Eyre farm) lies out of sight above the north-side plantation and gives its name to the brook here. In his classic *Highways and Byways*

Hazelford Hall looking across the Derwent valley to Bamford Edge

in Derbyshire (1905), J. B. Firth considered Highlow 'among the best preserved of the Derbyshire manors'. It was the sixteenth-century home of the remarkable yeoman farmer Robert Eyre and retains a fine staircase, a gateway adorned with ball finials and a stone dovecot at the edge of the fields.

The stream that rises near Abney village, above the thousand-foot contour on Abney Moor, flows down the tributary Abney Clough to join the Bretton Brook at Stoke Ford.

Bretton Clough is now uninhabited, but far into the nineteenth century it was a centre of moorland agriculture and pasturage. There were five farms in the dale, all long since fallen into ruin. Gotheredge Farm, for instance, was erected in the seventeenth century, high up the side of the valley near the dominant gritstone outcrop called Gotheredge. Its last occupant was a Billy Bingham, who left about 1865, after which date it became a barn. A murder took place at Gotheredge Farm about the year 1785. Two accounts of the crime exist: in one, 'Blinker' Bland, an Abney man, is said to have struck the farmer on the head with a milking stool, whereupon the terrified wife ran down the hill to the neighbouring farm in her 'night shift' shouting for help. The other account states that some masked men, including 'Blinker' Bland, entered the farm, and the farmer exclaimed 'Blinker! Blinker, ah know thee!' The men searched the house fruitlessly because the farmer had recently taken £400 to the bank. In their rage they murdered him, but his wife and child ran away and hid in the bushes nearby. The men were subsequently brought to justice.

The neighbouring farm to which the frightened farmer's wife ran that night centuries ago was, in fact, two holdings. It is remembered as Bretton Clough Twin Farms, now completely ruined not far below the fine gritstone outcrop of Gotheredge and a short distance above Bretton Brook. The eastern dwelling of the semi-detached pair was known as Fairest Clough Farm; it was a 'two-up and two-down' affair and was probably the original part. On the front door lintel was carved 'I M R 1782', a reference to either the Middleton or Morton family.

The western dwelling was called Hawley's Farm and featured the common flat-faced gritstone windows and door lintels of the early nineteenth century. William Hawley was living here about 1860, a corn merchant with a warehouse in Chesterfield. At that time the coming of George Stephenson's Midland Railway was still the talk of the town. Steam was still the wonder force of the new age, and one day on returning home from Chesterfield, William said to his nephew: 'Ween see what strength steeam 'as.'

So saying, he filled the kettle, made up a good fire and tied down the kettle-lid with a piece of wire. William and his nephew went into the yard and watched the progress of the experiment through the window. Their wait was brief because, to quote William on recounting the incident to a friend, 'All of a sudden, Bang went the kettle, an' it brok', an' shifted all th' fixtures i' th' 'ouse floor! Ba goom! Steam 'as sum strength!'

The nephew inherited Hawley's Farm and took on the corn business, and was eventually succeeded by Joseph Townsend, who often boasted that he had 'two houses and ovver 100 ackers o' land for forty pun a year rent, an' it were as dear as hell-fire at that!' When a new gamekeeper arrived on the moors above Bretton Clough just before the First World War, Joe took any pheasants he found caught in the rabbit snares. An old native recalled that, 'This were Joe's undoin', an' they shifted 'im for it, an' for 'is sheep gettin' on th' moors.'

Townsend left Bretton Clough Twin Farms during the Great War and died in 1927. One of the farmhouses was occupied as a cottage for some time, being finally deserted in 1919. Since that time these old farms have slowly decayed to their present ruinous state.

Some way up the dale stand the remains of what is usually called Clough Farm, though this may not have been its original name. Writing in 1935, G. H. B. Ward – the celebrated 'King of Ramblers' – remembered that this forty-acre hillside farm was vacated by Ben Bagshaw, the last tenant, in March 1893 and that the house contained four rooms.

This holding was deserted when a rabbit warren was created here on the southern slope of Bretton Clough in 1893 by the lord of the manor of Abney and let to London furriers and tie-makers, Jacob Brothers. The venture seems not to have been successful and after three years was taken on by another tenant. The warren lingered on until 1931 but all it seems to have caused was rabbit damage to nearby crops, and the demise of hazel trees (which had previously provided 'many bucketfuls of nuts every year') and of 'wiggins' (rowans). Here, too, several falls of soil and rock on the steep slopes above Clough Farm were attributed to 'the burrowing propensities of these rabbits'. Looking westwards up the dale from this point, you can see the picturesque 'sugarloaves' of a series of landslips a short distance away, evidence of the unstable shales here.

An old footpath climbs the rough ground of the former warren towards Bretton hamlet on its ridge-top, passing the ruins of

Nether Bretton Farm. The mullioned windows and large, open-arched fireplace here suggest an early seventeenth century yeoman's residence. Here, too, is a stand of old, wind-blasted sycamores that helps break the wind on this exposed hillside at 1,150 feet.

Nether Bretton is one of at least seven houses in Bretton which have fallen into ruin since the demise of lead-mining here about 1870. The old people of the hamlet used to claim there was a quoit pitch at the back of the farmhouse early in the nineteenth century, and that during the lead-miners' annual feast day a whole sheep was once roasted. The tradition that Nether Bretton Farm was a public house may have some substance, but if so it must have been before the Barrel Inn got its licence about the time the Sir William Road was created after the Act of 1757.

From this edge of the plateau we can look out to the north, across the almost hidden trough of Bretton Clough, to the conspicuous mound of Abney Low (1,138 feet) where stands isolated Cockey Farm. A local tale suggests this place got its name from two 'cock-eyed' (cross-eyed) men who had an altercation here. One said, 'Ah wish thou'd look wheear thour't gooin,' and the other replied, 'Ah wish thou'd go wheear thour't looking.' However true that may be, Cockey Farm is known to be the birthplace of William Newton in 1750. He was a carpenter's son who wrote poetry and was taken under the wing of Anna Seward, 'the Swan of Lichfield', who gave him the title 'Minstrel of the Peak'. Little of his verse has survived, though Newton rose to relative affluence as manager of Cressbrook Cotton Mill, beside the Derbyshire Wye.

Bretton hamlet lies a few hundred yards along the lane beyond Nether Bretton Farm. The plague that visited nearby Eyam in 1665–6 also came to Bretton and at least one victim was buried in Bretton Clough. In 1745 the farmers of Eyam drove their cattle into the dale to secrete them when Prince Charlie's Highlanders invaded Derbyshire *en route* for Swarkestone beside the Trent.

With the construction of the Sheffield–Buxton road after the 1757 Act, Bretton assumed greater importance. The Barrel Inn was a calling-place for travellers and carters and rendezvous for local lead-miners. When John Morton, the landlord before 1860, believed himself to be dying from dropsy, Old Man Moorhouse of Nether Bretton, an accomplished stone-carver in his spare time, helped him make his will. He also advised the invalid to 'go out and get some Broom Tea, and sup it'. This he did and lived a further twenty years.

About 1830 the hamlet had its own foot race, probably at the time of Bretton Feast. The course followed the road for half a mile from the Barrel Inn towards Grindleford. A spirited ram was chosen and covered with soft soap to make it slippery, and the runners had to catch it along the race course.

If we walk westwards from Bretton, along the windy, ridge-top road, we soon have a long view down the sinuous length of Bretton Clough. There are the little landslip hillocks and the quiet, shaggy woods. Far away in the east, beyond the hidden line of the Derwent, rise the greater gritstone moors and edges under a broad expanse of sky. Often in this sky above the dale are seen gliders from the Derbyshire and Lancashire Gliding Club, based at nearby Camphill Farm where Bretton Brook begins.

Only four miles away to the north of the gliding ground on Abney Moor lies Yorkshire Bridge spanning the young River Derwent right under Win Hill's eastern flank. Though the present bridge is not particularly ancient, there must have been a crossing here for many centuries, named after the fact that it carried the road from the Hope Valley into Yorkshire. The county boundary is only three miles away to the north-east at Moscar.

You can go straight up the fairly even eastern side of Win Hill (1,518 feet) from Yorkshire Bridge, a stiff pull up Parkin Clough and the coniferous plantation above that to end on the open heather moor below the topmost capping of gritstone. The ascent is 950 feet in two-thirds of a mile, quite a slope by Peak district standards.

Immediately upstream of Yorkshire Bridge rises the grassy rampart of Ladybower Reservoir's impounding wall, an impressive sight 140 feet high and 1,250 feet long. It holds back a maximum of 6,310 million gallons of water, part of the great Derwent Valley scheme providing water for Derby, Nottingham, Leicester and Sheffield. Ladybower itself is the wooded clough, or valley, used by the Manchester–Sheffield trunk road (A57) on its climb towards Moscar. The name of the valley comes from the Old English words meaning 'Our Lady's cottage' or 'shelter' – maybe of religious significance or perhaps the domain of some long-forgotten female overlord, or a family name, because the de Bowers were a Peak District family. The original plan had been to quarry the stone needed for the Howden and Derwent Dams in Ladybower Clough. A protest meeting was called in Sheffield in 1901, and the imminent threat to what was called at the time 'one of the most beautiful places in the Peak District' brought forth many loud objections. The plan was to remove huge quantities of

Fairest Clough Farm ruins, Bretton Clough

gritstone from the delightful, wooded valley, transporting the hewn stone by railway to the sites of the new dams. Further than that, the water authority would tip huge quantities of waste material during quarrying operations, so filling up the ravine below the great quarrying scars. Happily the protesters won the day, and the building stone had to be brought by rail from Bole Hill Quarry above Grindleford.

Few people really enjoy Ladybower Clough these days because so much of it is occupied by the sinuous A57 trunk road. Those who do meander through Priddock Wood and into Jarvis Clough or scramble up to the old quarry below Ladybower Tor on the northern slope will find an attractive corner of country, remarkably quiet considering the proximity of that busy road.

The Ladybower Inn stands beside this Manchester–Sheffield race track, erected about 1820 to replace the first inn which lay a little nearer Sheffield. The Cotterills were landlords here for a long time – more of a member of that family later.

From the airy summit spine of Win Hill there are really broad views. Especially good is the one to the south into the Hope Valley and beyond to the edge of the Carboniferous limestone country. To the north is the true grit country of the highest ground, broad brown shapes often blackened by cloud shadows. No wonder that Ebenezer Elliott – Sheffield's best-known poet – considered Win Hill a real mountain. Certainly it was a relatively convenient height in those days from which to contemplate the wild and untamed hills:

> His proud brow graced with that stone diadem
> Which Nature made ages before her practised
> Hand had graced with living gems the bluebell
> haunted shade.

On 18 March 1943 the outlet valve of Ladybower Reservoir was closed and the lower Woodlands Valley and Derwent Dale were flooded. When the villages of Derwent and Ashopton were inundated by the rising waters, many ancient farms were lost. Many of the inhabitants were re-housed in terraced housing at Yorkshire Bridge, downstream of the impounding wall, near Bamford. When King George VI formally inaugurated the Ladybower Works in September 1945 the valley floors had disappeared under the flood, and several lovely old farms remained just above the new water line but had been abandoned for fear of pollution.

If you take a circular walk from Yorkshire Bridge these romantic sites can be visited. First comes Ashop Farm, right under Win Hill's northern flank, with grand views across the reservoir to Ashopton Viaduct with the high, tor-topped silhouette of Derwent Edge beyond. This holding used to stand on high ground above Ashopton village but since the coming of the waters has sunk towards the apparent valley floor. Piled stones and a gritstone gatepost are all that remain. They were used early in 1985 as the foreground for a colour advertisement for the new Granada by the Ford Motor Company. Misty coniferous plantations and rugged hill-tops and lapping water: it all looked most romantic – and so it is, in the right lighting conditions. In winter, though, this 'other' side of Ladybower Reservoir (opposite that taken by the A57) is dark and dank because the low sun never reaches this far.

Further along comes Dryclough, appropriately named, where a tiny hollow without a stream seams the hillside (its conformation now largely hidden by the dense plantings of conifers). Beyond a curve in the shore-line stand the remnants of Nether Ashop Farm. Those who can remember travelling the A57 in early post-war years might recall seeing Nether Ashop across the reservoir, standing just above the high water level and looking rather grim. Smoke still issued from its chimneys in those days. Now, though, the farmer has long since gone, as have the house and buildings. All that remains are the wrought-iron front garden railings and laburnum tree which, in earliest summer, blooms as though nothing had happened. When the sun shines, the poignant golden blossom makes a glorious foreground for Rough Wood and Crook Hill's twin tops above.

Then comes Underbank Farm, again completely swept away. It stands opposite the mature beech and oak Grimbocar Wood which climbs towards Crook Hill's top. A mile further up the valley, beyond the head of the reservoir and now totally secreted by mixed woodland, stands the ruin of Elmin Pitts Farm (literally 'hollow where elm trees grow') where the Townsends were tenants. Old Man Townsend was noted for his parsimony: in an attempt to reduce the fuel bills, he shot up any loads of coal he brought from Bamford station at the bottom of the steep hill below the farm; as the women of the farm had to fetch any coal they needed up the slope, he thought this expedient would make for more efficient use.

The late Joe Townsend, well remembered by so many as gamekeeper and resident of Snake Cottage adjacent to the Snake

Inn, was born at Elmin Pitts Farm and had to walk three miles each way to Hope school, along the Roman road which reaches 1,050 feet at lonely Hope Cross. What a journey home for a small child on a dark December afternoon with the cold wind whining in the solitary, bent rowans!

The long arm of Ladybower Reservoir which stretches northwards for two miles up Derwent Dale caused the inundation of Derwent village; it also caused the demise of several lovely old farms which remain above the present shore line. One of these is grand old Grainfoot Farm, its tumbled stones still visible at the water's edge on the reservoir's eastern bank, below the long slopes of Whinstone Lee Tor. Teas used to be served here to ramblers; before that, foxhunters breakfasted here before turning out onto the high ground. Now the only visitor is the solitary angler who picks his way through the tumbled stones to a fresh spot along the shore.

Hidden in the conifers above this eastern shore are the ruins of Riding House. Shepherd Walker and his family lived here a century ago, and in the protracted severe weather of January 1889 his two sons set out to fetch in sheep stranded by deep snow high up near Whinstone Lee Tor. The young men were caught by an avalanche but their dog returned to the farm, and suspicions were aroused. Men went up to look for the missing men and soon found one of them, suffering from exposure but alive. His brother was later found in deeper debris – he was dead. Even here in Peakland's miniature mountain country avalanches can be a menace in certain conditions.

A last house worth noticing on the walk around Ladybower's shore stands just below the Manchester–Sheffield road near Ladybower Viaduct. It is best seen from the Bamford road on the far side of this viaduct, a square stone house with pyramidal slate roof. Miss Anne Cotterill lives here at Ginnett House, built in 1880 by her grandfather when he retired as landlord of the Ladybower Inn. His son went with his family to seek his fortune in the United States, and Miss Cotterill was born there in 1890. Nine years later the family returned to look after the Ladybower Inn, and when the grandfather died they moved to Ginnett House, looking out over the broad, green dale towards Yorkshire Bridge and Win Hill. Her father died in 1928 and her mother in 1939, and Miss Cotterill has lived here ever since.

When the new reservoir was being built, she was asked to move but firmly refused. The water authority could do nothing about it, though they had purchased the property, and so allowed her to stay on as a tenant.

'They didn't expect that I would live so very long, but I'm tough,' Miss Cotterill grinned when she told me the story recently. There is no electricity at Ginnett House, and the stable and cart shed lie under the water which now laps up to the fourth step of her front garden steps.

'We used to go down those steps and through the iron gate (now under water) to the old main road, to catch the bus to Sheffield,' she pointed down towards the reservoir. She hates the upstart lake before her, a sad reminder of the days long since gone when the view was one of tilted woods and lush valley pastures.

'The day I die they'll pull this house down,' she claims, 'but I'm going to live a long time yet.' Miss Cotterill has beaten a powerful water authority where other folk in these valleys have had to bow the knee and move away.

The main arm of Ladybower Reservoir fills lower Derwent Dale as far as the site of the old farm of Fairholmes, where is sited a National Park information centre and car-park. Cycles, too, can be hired here, the whole set-up well hidden by deciduous trees and judicious placing of grassy banks, which has earned the authority a conservation award. Immediately upstream of Fairholmes rears the gritstone bastion of Derwent Dam (completed in 1916 after ten years' work) and behind it 2,120 million gallons of chilly water when it is brim-full.

Howden Dam rears in just the same way above the head of Derwent Reservoir, its wall a yard higher (117 feet) but its water capacity slightly less. Come here to the top of Howden Dam when it is full and a northerly wind sends white-topped waves crashing over the brink and foaming down the masonry overflow. Incidentally, a useless but interesting fact is that 1¼ million tons of gritstone came from Bole Hill Quarry to build these two twentieth-century castles. They rear now through their mature coniferous fringe; from afar they could be fairy castles but their coming, of course, spelt the end of an age-old way of upland life.

The narrow public road ends at the King's Tree, and just beyond it Linch Clough comes down to the reservoir's west bank. There are stepping-stones here, and a few yards above them stood Ronksley Farm where Joseph Tagg was born in 1867. This ancient farmstead looks a grand spot on a faded photograph taken prior to its demolition in 1910, when Howden Reservoir was filling up. Joseph Tagg was one of the best-known sheepfarmers in the southern Pennines and became a champion sheepdog trialist, selling dogs far and wide for large sums; he came to be best

Howden Reservoir from above Gores Farm

known, though, by way of his final going at the end of 1953. At the
age of eighty-six he had become forgetful and after walking a
dozen miles with his collie bitch 'Tip' he wandered up the
Westend Valley in the failing light of that December afternoon.
Maybe he had gone back to a childhood when he came this way so
often; maybe he was checking the flocks of sixty years before.
Fifteen weeks later, on 27 March 1954, his remains were found
at 1,525 feet on Ridgewalk Moor, and Tip, bedraggled and
emaciated, lay beside her master. Rescuers had several times
passed fairly close to this place, but no one had stumbled on the
little party, and so the faithful bitch had remained at her post. Tip
survived her ordeal and touched the heart of the nation. Now she
lies on the moors above upper Derwent Dale, this time forever.
Her memorial stands near Derwent Dam wall, a feature
well-known to passing walkers and motorists.

Ronksley Farm was just one of several farms of the upper
Derwent which went into virtual oblivion with the coming of
Howden Reservoir. Banktop Farm, though, remains on its hillside at 1,150 feet above the point where the Westend River
empties sluggishly into the reservoir. No footpath comes this way;
the roofless house and its buildings stand in splendid isolation as
they have for three-quarters of a century. I shall never forget the
silent summer's day when we first came up to Banktop: a tawny
owl floated off on broad, brown wings to the edge of the mature
mixed wood, and a handful of ewes with lambs moved off up
Banktop Hey towards the sunny sky. Empty places like this
produce their own magic; presences of the past still linger; we can
almost hear the lowing of cattle and the call of far-off children by
the brook.

There's little wonder that such places as the upper Derwent
emanate powerful currents of the past, for they were the centre of
long-established settlement, of monastic organization from the
thirteenth century, when King John granted the upper Derwent
estate to Welbeck Abbey in Nottinghamshire. From a strictly
preserved royal hunting ground the district became a civilized
and productive agricultural estate, centred on old Derwent
village.

A century ago (1886) a large part of the dale was purchased by
the Duke of Norfolk, and the area reverted largely to being a
strictly guarded sporting estate – grouse this time, not boar and
deer. Millward and Robinson have pointed out that, though the
Sheffield blast furnaces now 'reddened the night sky beyond
Derwent Edge' (*The Peak District*, 1975), this huge estate was as

jealously guarded for sporting pursuits as it ever was by the medieval stewards of the king.

Grouse shooting still goes on here but a large proportion of the high escarpment east of the Derwent is owned by the National Trust. Much of it, too, is open country and anyone can wander here unhindered (except on the few days each autumn when the guns take to the moors).

To get a magnificent impression of this elevated wilderness, I urge the reader to walk northwards from the King's Tree to Slippery Stones, where the old Derwent packhorse bridge was re-erected in 1959, and follow the route of the ancient packhorse and drovers' track to the north-east. It climbs by way of Cut Gate to cross Howden Edge at over 1,700 feet *en route* for the Flouch Inn and Penistone beyond. Indeed, this was the main road for Peakland farmers visiting Penistone market, a lonely, moor-top route which gives the broadest views in clear weather. Away to the west spreads the great bulk of Bleaklow, giving away only a few secrets of its complex topography at this distance; to the east and north-east the slope dips gently for miles towards the valleys draining to the River Don and described in Chapter 1.

In summer this is skylark country; it is curlew country, too, and that bird's plaintive call is the epitome of all this elevated territory. You may make out the glint of traffic on the Woodhead road (A628) near the Flouch; you will probably be able to pick out the pencil line of the TV transmitter on Holme Moss over seven miles distant to the north-west; you will certainly see the slender tower of the TV transmitter atop Elmley Moor over ten miles away to the north. This latter is the substantial replacement for the lattice girder structure which collapsed in March 1969. It is 1,084 feet tall, the tallest concrete building in Britain, and weighs 11,200 tons. It is far enough from this high belvedere to be an attractive feature in the view.

Sheep and shepherding have fashioned most of the scenery before us. Hill farming has relied on the Pennine sheep as the backbone of its economy. Sheep are everywhere, and we can still see characteristics of the age-old breeds in the present animals grazing above the Derwent and on Bleaklow – the White-faced Woodland, (the Penistone) and the Derbyshire Gritstone make their mark despite increasing use of the Swaledale and other far-away breeds. Shepherding has left its mark on the landscape – and on the latest maps, too. A gritstone outcrop north of the Derwent, overlooking Hoar Clough, is called 'Shepherds' Meeting Stones'. These rocks were the regular venue for sheepfarmers, when stray sheep were exchanged and driven back to their respective walks. The rocks stand high and warm above the late summer heather banks but the shepherds no longer come up here to exchange lost animals.

3

Villages along the Line

When the Midland Railway Company decided to have a last fling and build a route between Sheffield and Manchester to compete with the Manchester, Sheffield & Lincolnshire Railway's Woodhead route, they chose the line of least resistance, the Hope Valley. Two long tunnels were required and it came into operation in 1894.

Totley Tunnel is the longer and at 3 miles 950 yards second only to the Severn Tunnel. Its construction under Totley Moss was dogged by inordinate amounts of drainage water and took almost six years in the building but steam trains finally came out of the western portal below the steep silver birch woods above Padley, and this part of the valley was never quite the same again. Those parts of the Derwent Valley between Grindleford and Bamford, and the tributary Noe as far as Hope (all popularly called the Hope Valley), became viable commuter country for Sheffield. No longer were Fulwood, Ecclesall and Dore the commuter limits – one could now live in the rural backwaters of Hathersage or Grindleford and travel easily to work in the city.

The wooded western portal of Totley Tunnel is actually at Padley though the little station there is called 'Grindleford'. That village lies some way down the valley side at the bridging point of the Derwent. All about Padley and Grindleford is evidence of the building boom occasioned by the arrival of the railway: tall, red-roofed, mock half-timbered villas stand in steep gardens, most embowered by mature trees. They climb up the eastern slope of the valley, and the highest situated of all is 'The Gables', built for my great-uncle Job Holland to a design by Lutyens. Amongst the original dwellings are modern affairs, mostly in local stone as dictated by the Peak Park Planning Board.

By walking beyond Grindleford station you cross the torrent of Burbage Brook where it issues from its popular gorge, and here stands the very old Padley Mill, long since become defunct.

Hathersage Church from the Dale

Wooden bungalows range up the slope beyond, the legacy of the tunnel-builders but now much improved and enlarged. The stony, unadopted road continues past a row of pre-war semis of unattractive countenance; they highlight the need for the present strict planning control on site and building materials. Beyond that again stands Padley Chapel.

Padley Hall was built in the second half of the fourteenth century, at some time before the heiress Joan Padley married Robert Eyre of the old Hope Valley family. Early in the sixteenth century Padley came by marriage to the Roman Catholic Fitzherberts and was occupied by John Fitzherbert in 1588, the year of a raid on Padley Hall by the Lord Lieutenant of the county when two Roman Catholic priests were found in hiding, and they and John Fitzherbert were taken to Derby gaol. The priests were put to death later that year, and John Fitzherbert died (maybe from prison fever) in a London gaol in November 1590.

At a later date the Hall became a ruin, and the impressive gatehouse was used for a long time as a barn. In 1933, when a survey of the site was undertaken, the distinguished medieval historian Sir Harold Brakespeare discovered the stone table of the altar of the original chapel. The gatehouse was restored and the altar stone replaced inside (the east end of the first floor was the original chapel). It is now called Padley Chapel and is the scene of an annual Roman Catholic pilgrimage every July. More interesting than the old gatehouse, though, are the ruined foundations of the Hall with its spiral staircase, original circular hearth in the middle of the great hall and sloping, stone-flagged courtyard.

High on the hill behind Padley Chapel are the remains of Bole Hill Quarry from which were extracted 1¼ million tons of gritstone to build Howden and Derwent Reservoirs at the beginning of this century (see Chapter 2). Silver birches have worked a miracle and completely hide the scars. All the land beyond and behind Padley is, in fact, part of the National Trust's Upper Padley estate; it is a pretty dale-side of sheep pastures and mixed woodland. You may walk towards Hathersage beside the broad waters of the Derwent, Peakland's major river, or higher up the slope through those grand old woods.

The railway traverses the slope through these woods, as lovely a couple of miles of rail journey as any in England.

Beyond the woods to the north-west lies Hathersage, gateway to the Hope Valley for most road-users from the Sheffield side. What with the main road and the railway it was inevitable that this busy little village should grow its crop of commuter homes early this century. They are largely Edwardian and stone, ranged

Padley Chapel, near Grindleford

up steep hillsides less wooded than at Padley and Grindleford. The old heart of the village is in 'The Dale', the little valley running up towards Stanage Edge and overlooked by the parish church of St Michael, described by Pevsner as 'typically Derbyshire'. A steep lane climbs from The Dale to the church, passing behind the heavily rusticated and rather ridiculous Rock House, a thing straight out of the Tuscan hills and quite incongruous here in upland England.

Hathersage is Charlotte Brontë's 'Morton' in *Jane Eyre*. She was a friend of the vicar and his sister, the Nusseys, and came to stay with them in 1845. Here at the heart of the village she must often have come across the common local surname Eyre, and so it is not surprising that she chose it for the name of her heroine. High above the village, to the north-east, stands romantic Moorseats in its old-world garden, the model for 'Moor House', home of Charlotte Brontë's St John Rivers' and his sisters. The house exudes true antiquity; it has the spirit of its place, halfway between green valley and blasted moor. Part of the building may date from the thirteenth century, some is certainly seventeenth century, and there are additions of 1857. Until the Misses Hodgkinson left, only a few years ago, Moorseats retained all its old-time atmosphere, stone flagged floors and all. Modernization does not do these really old places any good at all, though life may be made cosier.

Industrialization came to Hathersage early last century. There are two mills from this period, built in The Dale below the church and at the lower end of the village, which produced needles, metal buttons and steel wire.

The greatest asset this place has, though, is its attractive siting on steep slopes above the main valley. The view from Ninelands Road, for instance, up the Hope Valley to Lose Hill, the Great Ridge and the dark bulk of Kinder Scout beyond could hardly be bettered from any residential area within the Peak District. No Sheffield commuter could ask for a finer, more balanced prospect from windows or garden.

But there is one blot on the view – a relatively recent residential development above Jagger's Lane and Cogger Lane, high up to the north-west of the village proper. It is clearly visible in that lovely Ninelands Road vista. However permission was obtained for this quite unnecessary post-war estate of detached houses on a most conspicuous ridge-end position in the National Park defies understanding. The building materials have mellowed somewhat, and hedges and garden trees have helped to hide this nasty scar but it still deserves its local name of 'shanty town'. At night, I must confess, the twinkle of lights on this steep hillside is surprisingly attractive, evocative to some of a Pennine mill town, to others a fishing village above a Riviera coast.

Millstones at Lawrence Field, above Padley

The railway line runs due north-west for two miles beyond Hathersage station, parallel with the meandering Derwent and the main valley road. Then comes Bamford station, half a mile from the hillside village it is meant to serve. The River Derwent comes down from its upper valley here, to join the tributary Noe at Mytham – literally 'meeting of the streams' – Bridge. Before the bridge there was a ford, a very important one for those times as it was the river crossing for the Roman route between Navio, a fort at nearby Brough, and Templeborough in the Don Valley. An eminent Roman historian believes the road then went up the present Saltergate and across deep-set Hurst Clough. This attractive side valley lies in that neglected quarter between Hathersage and Bamford.

Hurst Clough Lane winds up through its leafy cutting with ancient tree roots gripping dispersed and shaly strata before coming to Nether Hurst, an ancient cluster of farmhouses and buildings. Until recently this hamlet lay unspoilt and dreaming on its sunny hillside high above the busy floodplain. The Daltons moved away and the antique flavour is in danger of being lost on the altar of modernization, as has happened up the slope at Gatehouse. (However, the alterations at the latter hamlet are tasteful, never garish, and the paint is much in sympathy with the building stone.) The Roman Road may well have climbed by Gatehouse and up towards Stanage Edge, crossing the watershed at 1,400 feet to continue eastwards as the Long Causeway – the medieval paving stones are still visible on the way down to Redmires Reservoirs.

Just above Bamford's rather inconvenient railway station lies Saltergate, already mentioned. The name originated from its use by pack animals carrying salt out of Cheshire *en route* for the east. Before that, of course, it may well have been the Roman road to Templeborough. The arrival of the railway encouraged the development of lower Saltergate, where several blocks of stone villas went up at the turn of the century, convenient for Bamford station. The subsequent development higher up the western side of the lane is unfortunate because large brightly painted modern houses do not marry in any way with the adjacent fields and Sickleholme golf course. These pale cubes of dwellings are conspicuous from far away in many directions – Sheffield's affluent suburbs seem to have leap-frogged far into the Hope Valley.

Bamford's brightest jewel is probably Butterfield's parish church of St John the Baptist of 1861, unlike any other Derbyshire church with its slender tower and extra-sharp spire above the main road climbing through the village and on towards Ladybower Reservoir and upper Derwent Dale.

The Hope Valley continues westwards where the Derwent comes down from the north to collect the River Noe near Mytham Bridge. Near this confluence is the settlement once known as Nether Shatton (Shatton means 'a farm in a corner of land', where the Overdale Brook comes down to the Noe–Derwent confluence) and now called simply Shatton. There are some lovely remnants of farmhouses and buildings near the ford on the Overdale Brook, almost entirely tidied up and rather too correct for comfort. The Homestead is perhaps the loveliest dwelling and the ancient barns nearby have been tastefully converted for human occupation, showing just what can be done when wealth and taste combine; which is more than can be said for the out-of-character rash of brash modern houses which line the road up from the river crossing and into the village. This invasion began before the last

Converted barns, Nether Shatton

war and has continued into recent times, largely a consequence of the motorized commuter, not of the railway commuter.

The same thing applies at Thornhill, former pretty upland hamlet at 700 feet above sea-level on the south-east ridge of Win Hill. Most of the attractive stone farms and cottages have been taken over and 'done up' with an exuberance of white paint, the *pièce de résistance* being, I think, Ryecroft Farm. Acres of shining white paint cover some of Peakland's loveliest old dwellings; the owners seem blind to the subtle beauties of shades related to the stone of which their places are constructed.

Hope's railway station, like Bamford's, is a good step from the village. The line follows the River Noe into the narrowing mouth of the Vale of Edale, between Win Hill and Lose Hill. Most of Hope village stands on the level land between the Noe and its tributary the Peakshole Water which comes meandering down from Castleton.

The effect of the railway is less obvious here: fewer late Victorian and early twentieth-century houses were built here, though the giant cementworks less than a mile south of Hope relied heavily on the presence of its branch line up to recent years. The out-of-character row of town villas alongside Castleton Road is a direct consequence of the cement works.

Until the railway came through the Vale of Edale, that broad and relatively fertile trough was undiscovered. The inhabitants ventured rarely to the world beyond their immediate hillsides. Most of the old houses and farms lie on the southern flank of Kinder Scout, above the frost pockets of the valley floor and in the best place to catch winter sunshine. The few farms which occupy the northern slopes of Lose Hill, Back Tor and Rushup Edge get little sunlight, and not without reason is this called Cold Side. The old established hamlets ('booths') which collectively make up Edale stand in favourable places, catching winter sunshine and with a reliable supply of water. Nether or Lady Booth, Ollerbrook Booth, Grindsbrook Booth (the main village), Barber Booth and Upper Booth are the names of these hamlets, each of which remains attractive, not violated to any great degree by the arrival of the railway. Edale was just too far for Manchester and Sheffield commuters to settle in any large numbers. Then, west of the station, the line enters Cowburn Tunnel *en route* for Chinley and New Mills, passing under Colborne Hill with the deepest air vent of any British railway tunnel.

4

Highest City's Leafy Edge

No large British city is closer to fine upland scenery than Sheffield, set upon the eastern flanks of Peakland's gritstone moors. In fact, this is Europe's most elevated large city, for its western boundary reaches 1,500 feet on Stanage Edge – no other comes close to this altitude.

As mentioned in an earlier chapter, the belvedere at Cliffe House Farm, near Bradfield, has been called 'the choicest surprise view of dale and moor within six miles of any large industrial city', by G. H. B. Ward, but there are many equally fine vistas within a mile or two of Sheffield's built-up western fringe.

Sir John Betjeman considered Broomhill the finest suburb in the country on account of its contours and leafiness. Many parts of this former steel city are in their own way the equal of Broomhill. Take, for instance, the village of Dore, four miles south-west of the city centre. Until 1934 it lay on Derbyshire's northern boundary but in that year it was transferred to the city of Sheffield; it is today a leafy, southern suburb.

Dore's old heart, around the parish church, lies at 650 feet above sea-level but parts of the settlement reach 800 feet and more – some of the highest city suburbs in Britain. The ground continues to rise towards the west, sloping up to the Burbage and Hallam Moors within the National Park. Below the village the land slides down eastwards for a mile to Abbeydale, where the River Sheaf runs towards the city centre.

One of the tributaries of the Sheaf is the Oldhay Brook, which used to form the important boundary between the kingdoms of Northumbria and Mercia, Dore lying just inside Northumbria. So it was that King Ecgbert came with his army at the end of his Mercian campaign in AD 829 and, just north of the border, met King Eanred of Northumbria at the place now known as the King's Croft. The Anglo-Saxon Chronicle records that Eanred offered the Mercian king obedience and allegiance 'and with that

Ecgbert Stone on Dore village green

they separated'. It was the beginning of a united kingdom, and the recently erected Ecgbert Stone on the village green records the event of nearly twelve centuries ago.

Like most villages, Dore had a good proportion of 'characters' in earlier times, and the best known of them was the schoolmaster

Richard Furness. He came from the plague village of Eyam in 1821 and is remembered as an amateur poet of some distinction. For thirty years he wrote a hymn every Christmas and was a prodigious, though lesser, poet whose verse was finally published posthumously in 1858. Furness seems to have busied himself with a wide range of duties, including drawing up building plans, blood-letting for the sick, drawing teeth, oboe-playing in church and painting signboards and names on cart sides. The old village school, to the north-east of the churchyard, was erected by public subscription in 1821, so Furness would have been set on to occupy this new building.

The many-talented Richard Furness designed the new Christ Church, built in 1828 to replace an old chapel. At that time Dore still formed part of the ancient parish of Dronfield but in 1844 its own parish was created. The new church has a rather plain, grim exterior of grey stone but the fringe of surrounding trees has done a lot to mellow it. The east window of 1902 is a memorial to Queen Victoria and commemorates the coronation of Edward VII, too.

When Furness died, in 1857, Dore was still very much a rural village on high ground above the Sheaf Valley, surrounded by tilting hill pastures and with many farms and stone cottages clustered within the settlement. Christ Church had its 'knock knobbler', a man with a long stick employed to poke dozing members of the congregation into consciousness. His other duty was to eject dogs with a pair of tongs. 'Owd Revitt' lived in the village in the last century, an eccentric artist who had a pet pig which walked round with its master. Revitt was a resourceful sort; he played the church harmonium and, when the leather bellows collapsed during a service, mended the leak with a lady chorister's garter! The story goes that he made a set of false teeth for himself but they rubbed his gums and caused the onset of cancer, which finally killed him.

The original railway route to Sheffield came by way of Rotherham; it was a branch line and caused much inconvenience to citizens. Settlements in and above the Sheaf Valley, to the south-west of Sheffield, remained relatively isolated. On 1 February 1870 the Midland Railway at last opened its direct line between Sheffield and Chesterfield through the Sheaf Valley but the nearest station to Dore was to the north at Abbey Houses (later called Beauchief). The local inhabitants now protested and demanded a station for themselves. Among the raised voices was that of the Duke of Devonshire, owner of large portions of land in the area, and he saw its potential for building purposes.

Exactly two years after the opening of the new railway, Dore and Totley station came into service, with half a dozen weekday trains and three on Sundays. This date, 1872, marks the beginning of Dore's metamorphosis from country village to residential suburb. For some time the development was piecemeal because only the Duke of Devonshire allowed his estates to be built upon – other landowners held on to their land for various reasons, ranging from resentment of urban sprawl to shrewdness in waiting until building-land prices rose higher. A new road was constructed up the hill, linking the railway station in the valley bottom to the old village centre. It was named Dore Road, and on both sides of it large stone residences were erected after 1880 as homes for Sheffield businessmen, convenient for the short rail journey to work. The effect of the new railway link is obvious when we compare Dore's population of 1,096 in 1871 with 1,656 in 1911.

Only as this century opened, and particularly after the Great War, did building begin on the undeveloped pockets of farmland surrounding the Devonshire properties. These brick and stucco, often semi-detached dwellings are in contrast to the heavy opulence of the Victorian stone building surge. In remote corners of the parish, too, there was development, usually in the form of large mansions for the wealthy who could afford personal horse-drawn transport up and down to the railway station. Some of them owned the first cars in the district, so could drive directly to Sheffield. One such mansion is Dore Moor House, one of the

Dore Moor House

largest twentieth-century houses in the Sheffield area. It was built in 1906 after a design of Lutyens and occupies a rather bleak site at 750 feet above sea-level, so is one of the highest and western-most houses in Dore. Extensive tree planting now shelters and enhances the site, home of a succession of steel magnates. More recently Dore Moor House was the guesthouse for a large steel-making organization and now – a sign of our more frugal times – it has been divided into several luxury apartments.

High on the edge of the village, above Strawberry Lee, we can look in fine weather over this delightful countryside and still imagine ourselves deep in rural England. In fact, we are but a stone's throw from one of Sheffield's most affluent suburbs. That is one of the great attractions of Dore and other western villages-cum-suburbs. Eanred and Ecgbert (even Richard Furness) would have been hard pressed to make anything of the delicatessen, Indian restaurant and flower shops but they would have found the views over the surrounding hills and dales still quite familiar.

The original bridle road from Sheffield via Dore to the Derwent Valley climbed up and down by Whirlow Hall Farm, Limb Lane and Dore Townend and snaked across shady Meg and Jin Hollow. This latter is said to have been named after two sisters, Margaret and Jane, who were lost in a snowstorm and found here in each other's arms when the snow melted. The bridle road continued up the hill, vaguely parallel with the present main road, and came at last to Fox House at the now busy road junction (A625 and B6055). It was probably built after 1773 by George Fox (who died in 1821, aged ninety-three), of the Callow Farm family, near Hathersage. It was then simply a one-up, one-down shepherd's cottage with a small outbuilding. It became an inn about 1816, when the 'new' road was built – the date on the parapet of Whirlow Bridge is still visible – to replace the original route. George Fox had the sheep grazing off the nearby Burbage Valley, and his shepherd would live at the little cottage.

The dukes of Rutland built their imposing Longshaw Lodge down the slope to the south-west of Fox House, and the 1757 Sheffield–Buxton turnpike road which passed right beside the new lodge was moved away to its present route, nearer Burbage Brook. The Duke also had the original crossroads at Fox House altered. If you look over the wall opposite the public house, the original line of the road can still be seen, despite the plantation of trees upon it. The new route was moved downhill so that now there is a complicated, and quite unsafe, staggered junction.

In July 1927 the Duke of Rutland put his Longshaw estate on

the market, offering 11,533 acres with 2,200 acres of additional sporting rights. The Lodge had eleven principal bed and dressing-rooms, and twenty-eight other bed- and dressing-rooms. Sheffield Corporation bought 3,210 acres and the Lodge two weeks before the auction was due to take place; most of this was retained for 'water-gathering purposes' but the Lodge and 747 acres were sold to J. H. Doncaster 'and other Sheffield gentlemen who intend to present the property to the nation through the National Trust'. Fox House Inn and an adjoining cottage and 9½ acres were sold to a local brewery for £5,500 and the Chequers Inn (below Froggatt Edge), a cottage and 11½ acres fetched £3,600. Longshaw Lodge remains a National Trust property, divided into luxury flats.

Running roughly parallel with the present (1816) road from Whirlow Bridge to Fox House is the 1757 Sheffield–Buxton turnpike. It keeps to higher ground further west. It climbed up the ridge from Ecclesall, another attractive western city suburb, to the hamlet of Ringinglow, then branched south-westwards to mount the edge of lonely Burbage Moor, reaching 1,392 feet on Houndkirk Moor. Here are the remains of Bage Field, where oats were grown in the hope of producing grain for grouse on the Longshaw estate early last century – something of a hopeless task in an average season at this elevation! This 1757 turnpike is a worn-out, stony track now and one of the best old roads still in existence in the district. It gives the walker some idea of the problems of travelling inhospitable country in the eighteenth century.

Ringinglow was the burial place of some long-forgotten chieftain: his 'low' or burying place was a heap of stones near the little chapel near the source of the Limb Brook, but a short time before 1574 a local man called Thomas Lee is known to have 'taken and led away a great sort of stone'. So much for sixteenth-century interest in prehistory! The mound has gone forever but the place-name remains. The best-known building here is the conspicuous octagonal Round House, built in 1795 as a tollhouse on the Sheffield–Buxton turnpike. Up to a few years ago, if you tapped on a downstairs window, it would be opened and you could order refreshments; but that service has passed into oblivion. Across the road, though, is the battlemented front of the Norfolk Arms public house dating from about 1840 but known to have existed in one form or other for five centuries. In the broad hollow of the infant Limb Brook below Ringinglow the coal measure shales lie exposed above the gurgling waterway. Here, in the eighteenth century, green vitriol was worked – hence the name of the now ruinous Copperas House Farm. There were several small coal-mines close to Ringinglow, abandoned about 1862, and a busy wiremill started by Robert Cooke of Hathersage in 1844, operated for only thirty or so years. The attractive assemblage of cottages opposite to Round House maybe owe their existence to the opening of the wiremill.

The road continuing westwards beyond the hamlet is the old turnpike to Manchester via Burbage Bridge and the Hope Valley. The breezy moor over which it mounts to the skyline has been called dull but many hardened ramblers never find it so. G. H. B. Ward describes it as 'traversed by crisp winds, and though there is a sombre colouring, the great gentle sweep of the moors up to Stanage Pole in the distance is impressive'.

A level lane runs towards the north at Ringinglow, too. This traverses the foot of the wild Hallam Moors and gives magnificent views into the verdant Mayfield Valley immediately to the east, with the busy cluster of more Sheffield suburbs all around it. There is Lodge Moor, Hallam Head and affluent Fulwood with the white tower of Hallam Tower Hotel three miles distant above the trees; and the great, grey mass of the Royal Hallamshire Hospital and the Potala-like bulk of Hyde Park council flats far away beyond the city centre. From this distance amongst the encircling trees it all looks most romantic.

Muriel Hall of Fulwood has written several fascinating local histories centred on the Mayfield Valley. They are full of stories from the past and show just how swiftly a rural district can change – the old farming families and semi-remote settlements have virtually gone; rashes of housing estates have crept ever nearer to the fringes of this grassy dale; most of the cottages and farmhouses are 'improved', their dung-heaps and scratching hens replaced by gravel drive and snapping poodles.

Carts trundled their grindstone loads from Stanage Edge, along the stone-flagged Long Causeway and down into the pretty, wooded hollows like the Mayfield Valley. These declivities rang to the sound of water-driven hammers, and sparks flew from workshops where 'Little Mesters' put an edge on scythes, sickles and billhooks. All that quiet industry has gone, remembered in one or two places with working museum-pieces like the Shepherd Wheel beside the Porter Brook, in the lower Mayfield Valley below Fulwood. This delightful stream tumbles eastwards off the Hallam Moors into this pretty valley where narrow lanes fall and climb between the encircling ridge-top suburbs.

One of these is Cottage Lane, near Whiteley Wood. In a hedgerow nearby is a pink marble water-trough supported by a dozen round marble legs. A closer inspection reveals an inscription to the memory of Henry Wilson of Westbrook. He was born in 1807, a member of the illustrious Wilson family of Sheffield, snuff-manufacturers. He lived at Westbrook House, adjacent to the Shallow Vale Mills where the family still make their world-famous snuff. Henry's eldest son was a boy of eleven in 1843 when, playing in the garden at Westbrook, he was killed by a stone thrown by another boy walking by in Frog Walk. A weeping ash was planted at the spot and is still there. Another son, Alfred, was disfigured by a boyhood accident, never married and took to drinking claret. Henry Wilson died in 1880, and the marble drinking-trough was erected by his two daughters at the busy road junction of Hunter's Bar, not far from the snuff-mill, in 1901. One daughter married a Westbrook man-servant, and the other became a curate's wife and had seventeen children!

How, then, did the trough come to be relegated to a lonely hedgerow? When the roundabout was constructed at Hunter's Bar some years ago, the trough had to be removed and the city council finally placed it on one of their farms. The trough, then, still serves its original purpose when cattle graze these fields in summertime, which is a better fate than to have been filled with soil and bedding plants beside some busy highway.

Thomas Boulsover (1704–88) lived at Whiteley Wood Hall overlooking the Mayfield Valley. He invented silver-plating, which caused a rapid expansion of Sheffield trade. He built rolling-mills and a forge down in the valley so that besides silver-plating snuffboxes, candlesticks and tea-urns he manufactured saws, edge tools and cast iron. The two dams which still exist are the Forge Dam and the Wire Mill Dam; just below the former is a pleasant tea-room which opens right through the year, a happy venue for ramblers and families; beside the latter is a stone memorial to Thomas Boulsover, and the ruins of his works are still visible close by.

Though Whiteley Wood Hall is no more, its famous owner is remembered by the stone monument and the name of the woody hollow where it stands, 'Bowser Bottom'. Not far away are the elegant Edwardian houses of Fulwood's fringe, eloquent wooded slopes radiant in spring when drifts of daffodils shine as a foreground for the distant blue moorlands of the west.

Thomas Boulsover memorial beside Wire Mill Dam, Mayfield Valley

Magpie Mine, Sheldon

Black Holes, White Rock

Hundreds of acres of rolling plateau, mainly grassland divided by a lattice work of pale walls. Here and there a long line of woodland – plantation really – and pale-stoned farm buildings. This is the commonest face of the coniferous limestone area of the Peak District, west of the Derwent Valley. In bright sunshine this broad upland can take on rich colourings: green pasture, white wallscapes and blue sky above. So often, though, the limestone district is drab, bleak, uninteresting.

The dales eroded by rivers give some contrast to the blasted tableland but many of them have become heavily worn thoroughfares. Think of Lathkill Dale and see an almost endless procession of walkers and school parties armed with clipboards and pencils.

As far as I am concerned, the limestone district has a fascination for one specific reason. It is often overlooked that the Peak District has played a special part in the history of the development of geological science. The limestone attracted the attention of serious scientists from the eighteenth century, though Gervase of Tilbury had described, in 1211, a fantastic underground world where crops grew, far beyond the great mouth of Peak Cavern at Castleton. This latter has the largest entrance of all British caves and was used for a long period to make ropes.

In 1778 John Whitehurst's *Inquiry into the original state and formation of the earth* was published, and this set down for the first time the order of the strata of Derbyshire rocks and forecast what materials would be found in future mining operations. Eight years previously J. Lloyd was in the district and, having heard of the existence of a certain Eldon Hole, set out to find out more about it. His subsequent exploration produced a report which was the first accurate cave record, a lead not seriously followed up until A. E. Martel's book of 1895.

Eldon Hole is the largest open pot-hole in the Peak District, the mouth of its great shaft measuring 110 feet long and twenty feet wide at the surface. It lies at 1,383 feet above sea-level on the broad and grassy southern slope of Eldon Hill above the village of Peak Forest. Eldon Hill (1,543 feet) has the distinction of being the highest point of the entire Carboniferous limestone plateau of Derbyshire. Anyone travelling the Stoney Middleton to Chapel-en-le-Frith road (A 623) in clear weather can look north to Eldon Hill's grassy profile before the steep descent to Peak Forest and make out a shady hollow above a long, deciduous plantation. That is the site of Eldon Hole.

Lloyd learned that he was about fifteen years too late to explore the full extent of the pot-hole. About 1755, local inhabitants told him, the owner of the surrounding pasture decided to fill up Eldon Hole because several of his cattle had fallen down it. He employed two men to cart loads of stone to the hole but 'finding no visible effects of their labour, after having spent some days in throwing down many loads of stones, ventured to be let down into it, to see if their undertaking was practicable'. They reported 'a prodigious large cavern' and so 'desisted from their work' as it was obviously an impossible task to fill up the chasm.

Lloyd found one of the workmen who had descended into Eldon Hole and enquired whether there were 'any damps at the bottom'. He was assured it was quite dry so procured two ropes forty fathoms in length and eight men to let him down into the depths. For the first sixty feet he could assist himself with hands and feet but below that the rock jutted out and caused him difficulty in passing. As he went deeper, the rock 'was rather dirty and covered him with a kind of moss, and pretty wet'. Almost fifty feet from the bottom he swung clear of the damp wall and finally touched down almost 200 feet below the surface.

'There was light enough from the mouth of the pit,' Lloyd reported, 'to read any print.' He found down there two caverns, the one into which he had descended – 'in shape not much unlike to that of an oven' – and the other 'a vast dome of the form of the inside of a glass-house' with a small, arched passage from one to the other. This second cavern seemed immense and he guessed its diameter to be fifty yards, while, 'The top I could not trace with my eye but had reason to believe it extended to a prodigious height.' This larger cavern is actually ninety feet from floor to roof and is adorned with stalactites which Lloyd described as 'sparkling, of a fine deep yellow colour'.

The bottom of the shaft and the floors of both caverns were, of course, covered by a slope of loose stones. This was the result of the attempt of about 1755 to fill in Eldon Hole, and later

Eldon Hole

stone-throwers have added to the pile. This debris completely concealed the enigmatic 'second shaft'; a man living nearby subsequently told Lloyd that this shaft in the floor of the second cavern went down 'a vast depth further' but was covered up when the loads of stones were sent down. It was reported to have water at the bottom but Lloyd could find no trace of the shaft, and the pile of stones has never been fully excavated, so the fabulous 'second shaft' has not been seen since.

A local tradition concerning Eldon Hole gives weight to the existence of this 'second shaft'. Recommending Lloyd's explorations to the Royal Society in September 1770, Edward King FRS refers to the tradition in this way: 'Many years ago a poor old woman, hunting her goose, it fled from her and at last fell down into Eldon Hole, to her great sorrow; but for some days after she heard it was seen at the mouth of the Castleton cavern, and actually received it safe again from thence; the goose having, by fluttering of its wings, preserved itself from being dashed to pieces in its fall; and having found its passage safely through the subterraneous river.' (Sometimes this tale reports the goose emerging with plumage singed by 'the fires of Hell'.) Dye experiments this century have proved that water draining this part of underground Peakland re-appears at the Russet Well, close by Peak Cavern's mouth in Castleton. Whether a goose could ever reach Eldon Hole's supposed subterranean river system and progress for over two miles eastwards to the Russet Well must be a matter for serious doubt but Dr Trevor Ford has pointed out that, though the caverns of Eldon Hole have never been actual swallets (where surface streams disappear underground and enlarge underground spaces into caves), percolation water has weakened joints in the limestone. Experts consider the existence of a stream cave very likely deep down under Eldon Hole, and drainage towards Castleton is certain.

Edward King explained that, 'There is a large quantity of gritstone grows in the earth near Eldon Hole, but none near Castleton; and yet, on high floods, the river at Castleton washes great quantities of fragments of that very gritstone out of the mouth of Castleton cavern.'

Lloyd's problem now was to return to the surface. Fastening the rope round his waist, he gave the signal to be drawn up, which he found 'much more difficult and dangerous' than the descent. The rope loosened the stones above him, 'whose fall I every instant dreaded'. He seems, though, to have surfaced without serious incident.

His account was read to the Royal Society in February 1771, and when it was published in the *Philosophical Transactions* in 1772 five labelled diagrams of Eldon Hole were included. One of these shows the 'second shaft'. The Reverend R. Ward recounted the tale, in 1827, of a benighted traveller being 'conducted by two atrocious villains who undertook to be his guide' to the edge of the pot-hole and 'threw him headlong into this dreadful gulf'. Ward quotes Cotton's quaint verse challenging the passer-by to peep into the void 'and keep his hair from lifting off his hat'. If he does so, he is either bald or has sold his hair for 'more modish curls'.

This century has seen a great amount of quarrying for the high-quality limestone on the northern side of Eldon Hill, half the

Eldon Hill Quarry from Rushup Edge

hill now having been removed. Excavation continues. Eldon Quarry Cave was an enlarged joint-type cave with attractive stalactites but quarrying in the last forty years has completely removed it. About twenty years ago pot-holers exploring Eldon Hole reported blasting-smoke curling in its passages from the nearby quarry. Maybe the continuing destruction of Eldon Hill will finally reveal that long-lost 'second shaft' below this mightiest of Peakland's pot-holes.

Immediately north of Eldon Hill, below the quarried face, is the broad hollow called Rushup Vale. Best seen from the main road traversing the smooth flank of Rushup Edge between the top of the Winnats Pass and Chapel-en-le-Frith, it is really a series of elongated hollows where streams run off the shale and sink into the edge of the limestone. At its upper, eastern end is one of the largest swallowholes in the Peak District, Giant's Hole.

Water entering Giant's Hole swallet descends 600 feet to emerge at Russet Well in about four days and eventually drains to the River Derwent, though its initial drainage means that it would otherwise drain to the River Wye. The cave is classed 'Super Severe' and its full extent is 2¼ miles, which means that a party must take great care not to get into difficulties as rescue is hazardous along narrow passages and sumps. In 1956 a great deal of dam-building and pumping made it possible for cavers to explore more than two miles extra territory of this cave system.

Some distance to the south-east is the entrance to Oxlow Caverns, called by the first spelaeologists Rickety Mine. It is actually linked underground with Giant's Hole, and this combination makes it one of the deepest cave systems in Britain at 650 feet.

Come here to Rushup Vale on any week-end of the year and the chances are you will find parties of muddy folk, complete with helmets, lamps and slimy ropes and ladders. They are enjoying themselves in Giant's Hole or Jack Pot or Sheepwash Gullet, away from it all in the heart of the country. At the end of the day as likely as not you'll see them lying in a crystal stream, ridding themselves of ochre and mud and probably glad it's all over and done with for another week-end.

Space here for just one more story, one with a fairly dramatic end. Black marble was mined at Ashford-in-the-Water for a considerable time, a mineral much in vogue for decorative items and fireplace-surrounds in Victorian times. The River Wye provided water-power as it meandered down towards Bakewell, and while Ashford had plenty of water, its upland neighbour Sheldon hadn't enough. Ashford lies at 450 feet but Sheldon is at 1,000 feet on the limestone plateau.

Mining of lead at the Magpie and other adjacent mines allowed the local inhabitants to supplement a meagre income from farming on this porous plateau. Lead-mining also produced cash for a reliable water supply to the village, pumped up from the Wye a mile away and 550 feet below it. The Magpie is as complete a lead-mine as any you will find in the Peak District, with over twenty shafts and ruined buildings. The main buildings are now a field centre, and visitors can obtain information when it is open.

It may have been worked for three centuries and it is known that Thomas Woodruff and partners were operating it in 1795. Serious mining came to an end in 1883 but several half-hearted

Magpie Mine

attempts have been made since to work the mine. The great menace has always been water: that commodity so short on the surface at Sheldon drains away underground and caused a continuous headache for the miners. The main shaft is 728 feet deep, considerably deeper than the drainage sough level, so a pumping-engine had to raise water from the lowest 150 feet of the shaft for any hope of working at this new, lower level.

This drainage sough was carrying 8 to 9.5 million gallons of water per day from the mine to the River Wye below Great Shacklow Wood, a mile west of Ashford-in-the-Water in 1929. Then in 1962 a portion of the sough roof collapsed; not only did this make the mine inaccessible from this lower level but it blocked off the drainage water. Great pressure built up, of course, behind the blockage, and by April 1966 water was seen pouring out of the hillside in several places well above the sough outlet level.

Suddenly, on 23 April 1966, the pent-up forces burst out of the hillside, blowing a crater thirty feet deep. Hundreds of tons of stone and earth were sent flying, sweeping away the river-side footpath and almost blocking the Wye. For some time the river ran as a mass of liquid mud. The debris is still there to be seen at the foot of the steep wood but the sough runs free again, and most of Magpie Mine is once more drained of that troublesome water that Sheldon folk have found so hard to get at over the centuries.

6

Rocking Stones and Standing Stones

Stone circle on Harthill Moor

The River Derwent is joined by the Wye, its major tributary, at Rowsley, a stone-built village much enlarged when the Midland Railway came north *en route* for Manchester. The finest buildings here are the Peacock Hotel – hard by the A6 highway – and the old cornmill by the river. Spanning the river is the early seventeenth-century bridge with five pointed arches, easily missed by the speeding traveller on the highway. You can hardly miss the grand Peacock, though. It is one of the best-known hotels in all of Peakland and was built in 1652 by John Stevenson, agent of the Manners of Haddon Hall, which is less than two miles westwards along the main road.

A great boss of millstone grit rises to the south-west of Rowsley, covering the older limestone as far west as the River Bradford and the northern end of Gratton Dale. Looking at it from near Rowsley, the upland is well covered with hanging woods, and here and there a farm and a cottage peep out. It is fascinating territory, with two high villages, mysterious rock architecture and a concentration of prehistoric remains.

Stanton-in-Peak lies at 700 feet, facing west, a lovely stone village about a steep street with the church of the Holy Trinity near the top. It was originally built in 1839 as the private chapel of Stanton Hall, home of the Thornhills. It is quite an imposing building, inside and out, of good proportions, and contains interesting gifts of the Thornhills – especially good is the Italian bronze holy water stoup of 1596. The Hall lies back privately in its wooded park, a mixture of ages and styles. There is a bit of sixteenth-century work visible, a long range of 1693 and an entrance front of 1799. For two centuries it was the home of the Bache family, then it passed by marriage to the Thornhills.

Over the hilltop to the east stands Stanton Woodhouse, embowered in old trees at 500 feet and overlooking the Derwent. Like Longshaw Lodge mentioned in an earlier chapter, Stanton Woodhouse was a shooting-box of the Duke of Rutland, and it was described by Samuel Bagshaw in 1846 as 'an ancient Elizabethan house, situated on a fine elevation, surrounded with terraces, ancient yews, Spanish chestnut, walnut, elm and other trees, commanding extensive prospects'. Lord John Manners described those broad views from the house in verse beginning:

> Up Darley Dale the wanton wind
> In careless measure sweeps,
> And stirs the twinkling Derwent's tides,
> Its shallows and its deeps.

The house has been greatly altered but there are a few remnants left; the garden is an early Victorian gem – an intimate foreground for the far views down the Derwent valley towards Matlock.

A path slants up the slope from Stanton Woodhouse towards the hillside hamlet of Stanton Lees. There is a wealth of trees around, and views towards Chatsworth and the eastern gritstone edges beyond the Derwent. Again, we are reminded of Lord John Manners:

> The waving woods that crown the banks
> 'Bove Chatsworth's gorgeous pile,
> Repose in greenest gloom, nor catch
> The sun's departing smile.

A mile and a half to the south-east of Stanton Lees is Darley Dale, a long and straggling settlement astride the A6 trunk road. It can be separated into Two Dales, Darley Hillside, Churchtown and Darley Bridge. The traveller on the highway may not notice much of merit but there are some highlights if time is taken to look for them. At Churchtown, for instance, is the ancient parish church of St Helen containing the fine tomb of Sir John de Darley who died about 1330, shown here in a suit of mail and holding his heart in his hands. In the graveyard outside is one of the oldest trees in Britain – the Darley Yew – with a trunk girth of thirty-three feet. It certainly pre-dates the Norman origins of the church and may well be older than the fragment of a Saxon shaft discovered earlier this century, very rare because of its antique geometrical ornament. Then there is the wall painting of a ship which may be more than 400 years old, and the stained glass memorial window of 1860 by Burne-Jones and William Morris which depicts the Song of Solomon.

However, Darley Dale remains forever associated with one man above all others. Joseph Whitworth was born in Stockport in 1803. When he entered his uncle's cottonmill, he found the machinery very primitive and set about improvements, which involved his working for others in Manchester and London. Long hours and frugal living allowed him to produce his first invention – the true plane. He soon set up in business in Manchester, introducing the first standard gauges, taps and dies, planing-machines and the Whitworth thread for nuts and bolts. He became vastly wealthy and bought Stancliffe Hall on the eastern slopes above Darley Dale, enlarged by E. M. Barrie. Whitworth gave the village a cottage hospital and the rather grim Institute at the cross-roads. He is buried here at Darley Dale, and Stancliffe Hall is now a preparatory school.

Half a mile along the Matlock road beyond the Institute, St Elphin's girls' public school occupies the likewise grim, stone blocks of a former health hydro.

Back on the hillside the lane winds westwards round to Birchover, second village of this gritstone upland block. At Domesday it was recorded as 'Barcovere', literally 'at the birch-covered steep slope'. At its upper end is an extensive gritstone quarry, one of the few still operating in the Peak District.

Like Stanton this place consists largely of a steep main street with a grand medley of stone houses and cottages which modern architects seem quite unable to emulate. Birchover, though, exudes a certain romantic mystery, an air of other-worldliness. Is it the nearby gritstone tors that still house old-time spirits? Come here and make for Rowtor Rocks at the foot of the village.

'Rowtor' means 'rough tor', a tall jumble of gritstone blocks that rear suddenly up and give the impression of being man-made. In his *Pedestrian Tour through the Peak* early in the last century, Croston describes Rowtor thus: 'We came to an ascending path, leading to a narrow tunnel-like passage that winds between broken rocks . . . in some of the rocks, chambers or caves have been excavated; the largest of them has received the appellation of "The Echo" from the singular reverberation of sound that

Rowtor Rocks, Birchover

is heard within. Picking our way through the narrow intricacies – not without a feeling akin to terror, it must be confessed, for we could hardly believe that stones so carelessly put together as these are could be very secure.' The intrepid party continued to the top of the dizzy pile and found 'several blocks of irregular shape and somewhat less magnitude, and in the centre of this last group a stone pillar has been set up, from the top of which rises an iron rod that formerly supported a weather-cock, now destroyed'.

The steps cut in the rock are still there; so are the little tunnel and several small walls of gritstone blocks, and the topmost pillar minus its weather-cock. There is much evidence of former 'beautification' here, actually the work of the Reverend Thomas Eyre who lived at Rowtor Hall, at the south-western foot of the rocks, and died in 1717. He had a study up here on Rowtor Rocks and had steps and seats cut in the gritstone so that his friends could enjoy the broad views.

At an earlier time it was thought that Rowtor was the resort of druids 'and that these immense blocks were raised to their present position by their exertions, the several rocking stones having been objects of idolatrous worship'. Rowtor, is, of course, natural enough but may have attracted pagan priests as a place of worship – certainly druids have long been considered in the same breath as Birchover and these jumbled blocks. At the foot of Rowtor Rocks stands the little Druid Inn, famous now for its good food.

The rocking stones were a great attraction for earlier visitors, and the best one, a block twelve feet high, thirty feet in circumference and about fifty tons in weight, was described in the eighteenth century as being 'so equally poised upon one end that a child might easily give it a vibratory motion'. However, it is nearly two centuries since it vibrated because it was 'forced from its equilibrium by the mischievous efforts of a number of young men who assembled for the purpose on Whit Sunday, 1799'. Rural vandalism is not new!

Rowtor Rocks form an east-west ridge, and the mature trees, particularly beech and larch, give the pile a beauty which the Reverend Mr Eyre probably never saw. Through the trees are good westward views to Harthill Moor and far away to the limestone country beyond. Robin Hood's Stride and Cratcliffe Tor are conspicuous in that direction, a pair of further gritstone features.

Scrambling about the tor it is easy to see how a child in a school party recently fell to its death. The rocks are mossy, the drops from the perched boulders sudden.

Round to the south stands the Reverend Thomas Eyre's Rowtor Hall, now the rectory. The little church he founded – called the Jesus Chapel – is close by the lane under the rocks. After his death the house and chapel fell into ruins but were rescued and restored in 1869 by a Thornhill of Stanton-in-Peak. Adjacent to the Jesus Chapel lie a number of stone fragments from a Norman building which existed somewhere hereabouts – interesting relics.

Stanton Moor lies on the highest ground between Birchover and Stanton-in-Peak, typical gritstone heather moor interspersed with small tors and round-topped rhododendrons. The easily worked rock led to a lot of quarrying activity here, and there is, remarkably, still one quarry producing good-quality stone just above Birchover. At the eastern edge of the moor, overlooking

Stanton Lees and the Derwent Valley, stands the square tower built by the Thornhills in 1832 in honour of Earl Grey and his Reform Bill on land which is now (twenty-eight acres of it) owned by the National Trust.

This moor has more to offer than just the simple tower. In the 1920s and thirties the Heathcote family of Birchover excavated stone cairns in an area remarkable for the many burial and ritual monuments which survive from the Early Bronze Age (2000–1400 BC). An area of 150 acres contains at least seventy stone cairns, several stone circles, ring cairns and a standing stone. The area was obviously used intensively as a cemetery and place of worship. Items recovered by J. Heathcote and his son, J. P. Heathcote, include beads of bone, fossil and faience, a ring of polished jet and small cups containing parts of cremations. Many things connected with the living (rather than the dead) were also discovered – flints and chert flakes associated with the preparation of food and animal skins. So far, though, no Bronze Age houses or fields have been discovered here.

For many years the finds were displayed by the Heathcotes in their private museum at Clee House, Birchover. Since the death of J. P. Heathcote many of the items have been transferred to the City Museum, Weston Park, Sheffield, and are normally on view.

From Stanton Moor-top or Rowtor Rocks more interesting features are visible, towards the western edge of this gritstone outlier. A mile due west of Birchover a conspicuous stone mansion rises enigmatically out of its girdle of old trees. It is Mock Beggars Hall, its wobbly turrets beckoning the visitor up the field path from the Ashbourne road (A524). On close approach one is bound to wonder if some grim guard dogs will alert the resident ogre; but we need not worry too much, for smoke has never curled from the chimneys of Mock Beggars Hall for this is nothing more or less than a natural tor formation. It has come to be known as Robin Hood's Stride because the distance between the two highest tors is almost seventy feet – the traditional length of the outlaw's stride!

A short way to the north the ground breaks into a fine vertical crag called Cratcliffe Rocks. It rises boldly from the sloping wood at its feet, and to one side sits a pretty cottage. The outcrop has some good climbing routes in an area isolated from other gritstone crags east of the Derwent Valley. Hidden at the foot of Cratcliffe, behind ancient yews, is the Hermit's Cave, which always filled me with a combination of dread and awe when I drew near as a child. The original hermit may well have come here in the

Robin Hood's Stride (left) *and Cratcliffe Tor*

fourteenth century and carved a bench and lamp niche for his bodily needs and an elaborate crucifix for things spiritual. Let an early Victorian traveller describe the spot:

> A rude archway admits to a cave or recess, which is said to have been excavated by some anchorite, who made it his abode. On the right hand, as you enter, is a crucifix about four feet in height, sculptured in bas-relief, on which is a figure of the Saviour; the features of the effigy are defaced, and the legs are broken below the knees, but in other respects it is but little injured. . . . Of the origin or purpose of this lonely cell nothing is known, nor is there any tradition extant to throw the halo of romance around it; it is generally believed, however, to have been the abode of a hermit or a place of pilgrimage. Perhaps some gloomy recluse, with mistaken zeal, may have made it his retreat; or perhaps some good and holy man, following the example of the pious St Kevin, has sought its wild and rocky seclusion, to escape the wiles and bewitching glances of his fair Kathleen.

What is certain, though, is that this cave was occupied in 1549 by a hermit who supplied five pairs of rabbits to Haddon Hall kitchen: 'Unto ye harmytt for ye brengynge of V Coppull of Counys frome Bradley to Haddon.' This Cratcliffe resident may not have been a holy man, simply a homeless vagrant who lived by his wits, for many caves of the region have been temporary or permanent homes for tramps or destitute folk, even into this century; maybe Cratcliffe saw its last genuine hermit long before the sixteenth century.

From the stony top of Cratcliffe Rocks you can look westwards across the grassy dome of Harthill Moor towards Bradford Dale and Youlgreave. It is crossed from north to south by one of the primary prehistoric highways of Peakland – the Portway, which can still be traced from the bridging point of the Wye at Ashford to Wirksworth. Its route can still be followed, in part by antique footpaths, in part by narrow lanes hemmed in by limestone walls. From Alport (at the confluence of Lathkill and Bradford near Youlgreave) the Portway zigzags steeply up onto Harthill Moor. The inconspicuous back of Cratcliffe Tor and Robin Hood's Stride lie over to the left. Far more obvious are the four standing stones remaining from the so-called Nine Stones Circle. They thrust out of the ancient pasture as probably the best prehistoric monument in the entire district (unlike Arbor Low they are still upright). These warm brown stones date from the Middle Bronze Age and when one of them was re-erected before the Second World War it was measured at eleven feet eight inches, seven feet four inches of this being above ground. Standing here on a breezy day we can surely feel a strong affinity with the long-gone residents who toiled here to build this great circle under the blowing clouds.

About the same distance on the other side of the Portway lies Castle Ring, the earthwork of an Iron Age camp of which little has been discovered. A portion of the site has been broken down by generations of ploughing, and old stone farm buildings stand on part of it. The whole situation – humpy earthwork and large farm – exudes the aroma of great antiquity, little changed in this twentieth century.

From Castle Ring a field path falls steeply north-westwards through trees and open pastures towards the little River Bradford on the very edge of the pale limestone country. We are almost at Youlgreave and Alport on the winding main road to Newhaven atop the white plateau.

Saxon cross, All Saints Church, Bradbourne

7

Life on the Limestone Fringe

Where the great mass of Carboniferous limestone plateau gives way in the south-east to lower, gentler country, there is a district of attractive, green undulations, of small, grassy vales drained by winding brooks and peopled by a handful of unspoilt villages. Geologically it is a confused area, with shales and sands coming up against the older, harder limestone.

Several streams are born here at this boundary, swelled by subterranean water and flowing generally southwards to enter the Dove beyond Ashbourne. There are two major streams: the Bradbourne Brook in the west, the Henmore Brook to the east.

Several small streams come together to form the Bradbourne Brook; in the north-west is the tiny Bletch Brook which rises in a quiet, green dale below Alsop-en-le-Dale at the foot of the limestone plateau. No one knows how this stream got its name though it is of considerable antiquity, known as 'aqua de Blethche' about 1210. Alsop-en-le-Dale lies low in its tight hollow below the bare plateau-top where 'shivering clumps of ash trees' come late into leaf and are stripped by the first autumnal gales.

Half a mile to the west the Ashbourne–Buxton high road (A515) keeps to the upland at about 900 feet, but immediately one turns down the lane to the east there are trees and shelter and a friendly face to the landscape. Tucked into its tiny dale-head at 750 feet is Alsop-en-le-Dale. This hamlet (hardly a small village) was granted to William de Ferrers, Earl of Derby, and came soon to the Alsop family, who continued here for five centuries. In the mid sixteenth century the persecuted Thomas Becon, a chaplain at Canterbury Cathedral who fell foul of the established Church and was imprisoned in the Tower of London for his beliefs, came north to find peace. He discovered it here in this ideal spot as guest of John Alsop for twelve months. In 1688 the estate was sold by Anthony Alsop to Sir Philip Gell of Hopton.

What we see today is the largely Norman St Michael's Church, with traces of eleventh- and twelfth-century work – remarkable in this district and suggesting a fairly large population at that time, based on newly exploited local minerals. The finest feature is the Norman doorway on the south side but the west tower was only built in 1883 in a mock Norman style. The seventeenth-century Hall has an attractive symmetrical front which complements nicely the adjoining farm and buildings. What a relief that this bypassed place has not been spoilt. The little road is smooth now, of course, but it is not hard to imagine hens scratching on its former dusty surface or a line of ducks coming home from a day in the fields.

Two miles down that little road to the east stands Parwich, a large village of limestone farms and modest cottages. Like one or two other of the larger limestone fringe villages, it has been a thriving place for centuries, its Norman church of St Peter completely rebuilt in 1873 using some of the original features; the tall spire gives the parish church an importance beyond its size. The beautiful Hall of 1747 stands well with its back to the limestone hill, Parwich Hill, on the foundations of a house of 1561. It is tall, of brick and stone and not commonplace for the district, though Longstone Hall, Great Longstone, was built in the same year using similar materials. Its lovely gardens were created about 1905, and in 1931 it became the home of Colonel Sir John Crompton-Inglefield. Forty years later the Crompton-Inglefields departed for London but Parwich Hall remains a cared-for family home.

A nameless stream issues from the steep ground behind Parwich and trickles across the fields by Sitterlow Farm to join the Bletch Brook near the place where another stream comes down from Ballidon. This latter is almost a deserted village in a tiny dale-head hard against the edge of the limestone plateau, one mile east of Parwich. Eight hundred years ago it was a thriving village but it had gone by the end of the Middle Ages, and all we find today are four seventeenth-century farms, grand old places, and the much modified Norman chapel of All Saints alone in a field.

There is something special about quiet little churches at the edge of nowhere, and Ballidon has some of this magic. One thing spoils the English rural charm, though: at the head of the little dale beyond the last farm there is a giant quarry, eating still into the solid limestone reef of this plateau-edge. Dust, noise and a convoy of lorries in and out of that single, narrow dead-end lane – only its site in the confines of that little hollow prevents Ballidon Quarry being as big an affront to the senses as is Eldon Hill Quarry far to the north.

A short distance east of forgotten Ballidon is Hipley Dale, a sudden, small dry valley or gorge cut in the edge of the limestone mass and used by the Ashbourne–Bakewell road (A524). Clearly visible at the side of the road here are a couple of shallow caves with great mouths in the pale cliff. There are records of torrents of water suddenly bursting forth here after heavy rain, probably the unstopping of a former blockage in a cave system in the hills behind.

A major tributary of the Bradbourne Brook is the Havenhill Dale Brook, draining another shallow, grassy dale to the east with Brassington at its head, in a situation similar to that of Parwich above its own stream. Seen from the south, Brassington looks the limestone hill village *par excellence*, grey and stepped up the sunny slope, jumbled and tight-packed. It simply invites closer investigation.

At the Domesday Survey the settlement had the name 'Branzinetun', literally 'Brandsige's farm', whoever he may have been – maybe one of the Scandinavians who settled on these hills a good time before the Normans arrived. The early lead-miners who worked the bleak plateau to the north must have settled here in some numbers, near the Norman church of St James. Just wander around the village and see the variety of cottage architecture, and a splendid town-type house of 1615 complete with mullioned windows. An unusual thing to look for is the Saxon stone carved with a human form, hand on his heart, incorporated into the church tower by the Normans. He is high up and requires some searching for.

Though his view of the surrounding landscape has not changed as much as views from many English church towers, our Saxon mystery man will have noted the sudden metamorphosis occasioned by the Brassington Enclosure Act of 1803. Miles of limestone walls were thrown up on the dry hillsides and plateau behind the village. Modern change has come in the form of extra housing, though most of it uses appropriate materials and blends with the old buildings. What is to be deplored here, as elsewhere in the district, is the almost ubiquitous use of fancy, polished wood front doors in styles quite out of character with the buildings they give access to. The pleasing countenance of cottage or terrace house can be destroyed at a stroke by the inclusion of such a tasteless appurtenance.

The stream which rises at Brassington trickles southwards down a shallow, grassy hollow with its own footpath to Netherton Hall. Beyond this it is the Havenhill Dale Brook, and the old farm at Netherton is probably the Parva Bradeburne of 1361, by 1559 Lytle Bradbourne. Here in its empty valley the hamlet is dominated by the old house upon its knoll. In winter the grand aroma of silage is reassuring: life continues much as ever, and here are real people doing real work.

Immediately downstream of Netherton the stream enters the green confines of Havenhill Dale gorge, a constriction where steep Haven Hill (906 feet) swells close on the southern side. The constriction soon widens and the stream joins the Bletch Brook at an old cornmill adjacent to the Ashbourne road, close to a place where the lane to Tissington branches off to go through the water at what is probably Peakland's best-known ford.

Standing upon the crest of the spur immediately north of Havenhill Dale gorge is the next village, Bradbourne. At the Domesday Survey it was already 'Bradeburne', 'the broad stream', which must refer to the main stream to the east of the village. It is only a small village now and stands at almost 700 feet above sea-level, saved from bleakness by a wealth of trees near the Hall. This is a late sixteenth-century, three-gabled house standing back across a broad lawn adjacent to the church. The site is almost certainly that of the ancient manor of the Bradbournes. The Ferrers owned it later, and in Victorian times it had a succession of tenants. Now it is fully restored and still a private residence. A quaint little post office, cottages, working farms and the parish church complete the picture.

All Saints is of Saxon origin and there are bits of this early church in the north side of the nave. It must have quickly fallen out of repair, though, because a new one was built about 1130. The Norman tower is particularly fine, broad and unbuttressed and clearly visible from the Ashbourne–Bakewell road down to the west. As you enter the churchyard, the famous Saxon cross (about AD 800) stands before you, decorated with foliage and crude figures. It was broken up in the early nineteenth century, and parts were used as a gatepost and in a stile on the footpath to Ballidon. In his monumental study of Derbyshire churches Charles Cox suggested, in 1877, that the remnants be rescued 'from further maltreatment' and brought together again. This later happened and what remains is an impressive memorial to the first farmers of this pleasant spur-top settlement of the limestone fringe.

That other major stream of this district drains country further east, comprised of several tributaries which come together to form the Henmore Brook, Ashbourne's own little river. The main valley is broad and straight and relatively shallow, with the Scow Brook twisting down from its source on the neck of high ground just west of Wirksworth.

This is the site of the notorious Carsington Reservoir, approved in May 1978: its purpose is to make an extra 52 million gallons of water each day for the 2.7 million people in south Derbyshire, Nottinghamshire and Leicestershire. Much controversy surrounded the approval of this site as it was argued in some quarters that this extra water supply was not really needed at all. Local inhabitants and conservationists put up a brave fight against the permanent destruction of this broad valley, and the people of Ashbourne feared what might happen if the impounding wall gave way, as it lay directly upstream of the town.

Work proceeded to build a dam 1,250 yards long, using shale and a central core of clay obtained from the reservoir site. The stone facing for the upstream side of the dam came from local quarries. The dam wall has a maximum height of 115 feet and the surface area of the projected lake will be 750 acres. As work on the dam went ahead, two long tunnels were bored through the two ridges of high ground which separate the Scow Brook from the Derwent Valley near Ambergate. One tunnel goes under Alport Hill, the other beneath high ground near Kirk Ireton village. These tunnels have proved difficult and costly to construct, not least on account of very hard rock which caused the use of old-type hand-boring tools. The 5½ mile-long aqueduct thus created can be used to carry water to the Derwent for use lower down, near Derby or, in winter, for carrying surplus water from the Derwent to fill up the reservoir.

Then, suddenly, in the summer of 1984 part of the almost completed impounding wall collapsed because the weight of limestone being piled on it was too great for the underlying shale bank. Ashbourne folk were relieved that this had happened before the dam was filled and pointed to what might still happen if the work continued. An independent report published in the summer of 1986 suggested that it was still safe to proceed, and at the time of writing (Autumn 1986) the Severn Trent Water Authority intend to complete the reservoir by the early 1990s.

Overlooking the head of the valley are the twin villages of Carsington and Hopton, now bypassed by the Ashbourne–Wirksworth road. Carsington was a settlement at the Domesday Survey, its name probably derived from words meaning 'cress farm'; was watercress grown here in a tiny tributary of the Scow Brook? There is a nice little church here on the hillside with windows in memory of the illustrious Gells of nearby Hopton. At Carsington, in 1664, was born Sarah Tissington, who had no arms but became a well-known knitter, using her feet. Not long before this Joshua Oldfield was born here, son of the rector. He rose to be a famous Presbyterian minister at Oxford University. The village dos not have a great house but this is made up for at adjacent Hopton – literally 'farm in a valley'.

Hopton Hall

Hopton Hall has its back to the old road, bounded by a fairly rare crinkle-crankle wall in eighteenth-century red brick. Such high walls, bending in and out, are more secure than straight ones; vertical corrugations for fruit to grow against. The house was built in the sixteenth century by Thomas Gell, descendant of the Gells who settled here in the fourteenth century; they were landowners, farmers and lead-miners. In the eighteenth century the south front was much altered, resulting in the amazing (but attractive) segmental pediment looking out over the shallow head of the valley where the new bypass runs and, beyond it, the area of the new Carsington Reservoir.

The best-known Gell of the seventeenth century was the Parliamentary General Sir John Gell whose relics are still here in the Hall. Later came the classical scholar Sir William Gell who travelled widely on the Continent, settled in Italy and became a friend of Byron and Scott. He died in Naples in 1836. Other Gells stayed at home, one creating the road through the woods of Middleton a couple of miles north of Hopton and calling it romantically Via Gellia. The name has stuck to this day. Colonel Philip Gell farmed here until quite recent years, and his widow still resides at the Hall, sheltering as it does beneath tall trees at the foot of that broad limestone upland.

A narrow lane cuts cross-country from near Hulland on the Belper–Ashbourne road (A517) north-westwards to the Ashbourne–Wirksworth road already mentioned. It dips into and across the valley of the Scow Brook below the site of the Carsington Reservoir impounding wall and climbs through Hognaston on its hillside at about 650 feet.

If you pronounce aloud the Domesday name for the village, you will see how it has come down to us – 'Ochenavestun', perhaps 'the farm at Hocca's swine pasturage', no one can now be certain. The village is a grand collection of old cottages and houses and has broad views down the valley of the Scow Brook and Henmore Brook towards Atlow and Ashbourne. The parish church of St Bartholomew has a most wonderful Norman doorway carved with a galaxy of symbols. Pevsner suggests that they are 'utterly childish' but perhaps those far-off stone-masons had more oil in their lamps than we give them credit for.

Hognaston Winn is the 964-foot hill rising smooth to the sky almost a mile from the village. Across its broad top runs the Ashbourne–Wirksworth road, from where there are lovely vistas towards Bradbourne and Brassington and Parwich and the lime-stone upland behind them. This road (B5035) descends south-westwards off Hognaston Winn to the sheltered little tributary valley of the Kniveton Brook, a north-bank feeder of the Henmore Brook. Here, where the road dips for a moment before climbing towards Ashbourne, sits Kniveton, as nicely placed a village as any in the Peak District. It was called 'Cheniuetun' by the Domesday surveyors, and this is unusual because it means 'Cengifu's farm', and such a personal noun is feminine; she must have been quite a remarkable woman in her time to have left her mark so definitely here.

The parish church of St Michael has Norman origins (look for the round stone with a cross set in the nave wall – it may be Norman) and a thirteenth-century tower and stumpy spire. The Old Hall stands to the south, originally seat of the Knivetons. Lady Frances Kniveton in 1572 presented a chalice and flagon to

Kniveton village

the church but a later member of the family, Sir Andrew, fell on hard times because he stood behind Charles I and had to sell off most of the estate to keep body and soul together.

Near the centre of the village is the post office in a grey house; its garden is a mass of bright colour in spring. In fact, Kniveton is well worth a long drive or walk to investigate: a generally unspoilt settlement right at the edge of the limestone country, a sort of borderland where the short hill pastures give way to lush dairy lands and wooded country which soon becomes part of south Derbyshire and the English Midlands.

Townscapes

It's lucky that many of the biggest settlements of the Peak District have not been much deflected from the basic function of a place in which to live and work; they have not sunk to the level of a sugary tourist magnet, as has happened to many towns in, say, Lakeland. These no-nonsense towns, such as Penistone and Saddleworth, remain unself-conscious, natural and imperfect and are in contrast to the semi-tarted-up towns, such as Bakewell, which have changed their main function in recent times.

Ashbourne

At the southern fringe of the Peak District this old market town stands in the bottom of the grassy valley of the Henmore Brook, above the 400-foot contour. It climbs up the northern slope, too, where the Buxton road comes down from the limestone country beyond. Two buildings dominate Ashbourne – the Nestlé Company's dairy beside the Lichfield road and the parish church of St Oswald across the Brook beside the road to Leek.

Church Street leads from the town centre to the church, a broad and level thoroughfare which some think the best in Derbyshire. Be that as it may, it certainly has a grand air about it, flanked by fine architecture; there are the late-Georgian, three-storeyed Clergymen's Widows' Almhouses forming a courtyard on the south side; nearer the church are the Owlfield Almhouses (1640) and Pegg's Almhouses (1669), also on the south side, and just beyond them what is probably the best dwelling in the district, the early eighteenth-century Mansion House of five bays, three storeys and a Tuscan porch. Here lived Dr Johnson's friend and contemporary Dr Taylor, who had been at Christ Church, Oxford when Johnson was at Pembroke. He became Rector of Market Bosworth, Leicestershire, and St Margaret's, Westminster, spending most of the winter at his London house and summers at Ashbourne. Johnson and Boswell were often guests at

Ashbourne, Church of St Oswald

the Mansion House, and Boswell recalls the sunny morning when he found Johnson attempting to dislodge a blockage of branches in the Henmore Brook at the bottom of the garden. He pushed and probed with a pole 'till he was quite out of breath; and having found a large dead cat, so heavy that he could not move it', he called to Boswell to assist. Being 'a fresh man', Boswell soon made the corpse tumble over the cascade and float off downstream.

The finest room in the house is the Octagon, built out into the garden at the back by Dr Taylor where, according to legend, he entertained King George III.

On the opposite side of Church Street is the old grammar school, a lovely gabled building of 1586 that fronts directly onto the pavement. The single schoolroom was panelled in 1885 with oak removed from the parish church. In Dr Johnson's time the headmaster was the Reverend William Langley, who was always at loggerheads with his assistant so that the number of pupils once fell to one!

Just beyond on the south side of the road is the parish church, one of the best in this part of England. Indeed, George Eliot extolled it as 'the finest mere parish church in the kingdom' and James Boswell went almost as far when he called it 'one of the largest and most luminous churches that I have seen in any town of the same size'. Though these two may have gone over the top with praise, St Oswald's is a beautiful building, especially so its slender spire of 212 feet, but standing near the valley floor it is not seen from far afield as it would be in a more commanding position. There is much to see inside, and the main churchyard gates facing down Church Street are of excellent wrought iron, about 1700.

In St John's Street, near the steeply angled market-place, is the unusually named Green Man and Black's Head Hotel, an old coaching inn where Johnson sometimes stayed. Back in the town centre it is timely to remember the local gingerbread introduced by French prisoners in the Napoleonic Wars and made here ever since. Then there is the town's own special brand of football, played by limitless numbers in teams drawn from either side of the Henmore Brook, the goals three miles apart; this rough-and-tumble frolic is played on Shrove Tuesday and Ash Wednesday.

Bakewell
Like Ashbourne this is a valley settlement, most of it on the rising western bank of the River Wye. In its favour is the steep ground where some of the best buildings stand and can be seen from the valley floor to good advantage. They include the old, though

much rebuilt parish church of All Saints, the seventeenth-century Bagshaw Hall and the Old House (now a museum) which is Bakewell's oldest remaining dwelling.

The discerning J. B. Firth said in 1905 that the town has few ancient buildings, and he was right. The place has seen much change and, being on the A6, has long been spoilt by a huge volume of traffic. Add to this the great numbers of visitors who for various reasons come here in both summer and winter. Bakewell is too busy for comfort nowadays; noise and bustle everywhere.

The river flows under one of the oldest English bridges and down beside the timbermill, then on towards the broad floodplain and Haddon Hall. It was not always so, of course. The town's name is first recorded early in the tenth century when, about 920, a fort was established by Edward the Elder to help recover Mercia territory from the invading Danes. There are remnants of the associated earthworks at Castle Hill, dominating the bridging point of the Wye east of the town.

The first record of a market is in 1254, though the place had already been a local trading centre for two centuries. In that same year a fifteen-day fair was granted, making it the longest medieval fair in the region. Bakewell might easily have become a spa town, for it has warm springs: a chalybeate well produces water at a constant 15°C through the year, and in 1697 a bath house was built over it by the Duke of Rutland. The eminent geologist White Watson (1761–1835) was superintendent of the baths but was best known as a sculptor. (He succeeded his uncle as proprietor of the marble mill at Ashford and rose to fame as the creator of marble inlays of geological strata which are works of art and now reside in museums or private collections.) The bath house still stands in Bath Street, generally ignored or unknown by visitors. Not so the Rutland Arms Hotel, which stands four-square at the town's centre, built overlooking the London high road in 1804 as a replacement for an earlier public house. When Jane Austen stayed here early in the last century, she could alight from a carriage in the main street without causing traffic congestion; no one would dare to step from their car at this busy spot today!

Bakewell got its own rather grandiose station when the Midland Railway built their main line northwards up the Wye Valley to Manchester after 1860. The Duke of Rutland insisted on a substantial building – complete with his coat of arms carved on the stonework – as part of the agreement with the railway company for the line to pass through his estate at Haddon. It stood rather inconveniently far up the eastern slope beyond the river bridge and was closed when the line was abandoned in 1967.

Buxton

Buxton vies with Cumbria's Alston as the highest town in England. Both stand around the thousand-foot contour and share an understandably bracing climate.

The Romans discovered the thermal springs and called the spot Aquae Arnemetiae. There are nine springs which bring a quarter of a million gallons to the surface daily, from depths up to 5,000 feet. The boundary between Carboniferous limestone and the darker shales and gritstones crosses the depression where Buxton stands, so the original settlement which grew up on the high ground near the market-place is largely a remnant of limestone construction. Only the old parish church of St Anne (1625) remains from this period. What we think of today as Buxton proper dates from the late eighteenth century, when the fifth Duke of Devonshire set to work to create a proper spa town at the foot of St Anne's Cliff. Most of this 'new' town uses the more attractive mellow sandstone quarried not far away.

Buxton is a topcoat colder than most towns of the Peak District; anyone who has walked its bleak streets on a grey winter's day will know what that means. The place is often cut off by snowdrifts because all main roads climb fairly steeply out of the town. Notwithstanding the spartan climate, the Duke commissioned the York architect John Carr to set about the first phase of work on a spa town to rival Bath. The Crescent was constructed in 1781 near St Anne's Well and facing into the steep hillside of St Anne's Cliff, not a very promising site but the placing actually works very well. The magnificent Assembly Room was housed within the north-east end of the Crescent and saw many glittering social occasions before becoming part of the Buxton Clinic and now the town's public library; this is surely the grandest county library in Britain.

After the Crescent came the impressive Stables, standing on higher ground behind and now the Devonshire Royal Hospital. The central courtyard was covered in 1880 by what was, well into the middle of this century, the widest dome in the world. A little to the west stands Wyatville's beautiful classical church of St John the Baptist of 1811; while he was doing this, he tidied up St Anne's Cliff facing the Crescent, criss-crossing it with serpentine walks and flowerbeds.

Buxton. The Crescent from St Anne's Cliff with the Old Hall Hotel (left), the dome of the Devonshire Hospital (behind) and the Palace Hotel (right background)

In the middle of the nineteenth century Joseph Paxton planned the open space west of the Stables as 'The Park', with expensive stone houses overlooking a large, central oval of grass. With the coming of railways from Manchester and the south, there was a need for more accommodation, and the grandest hotel of that period is the Palace, built near the twin rail terminals in 1868 and once described as 'ornate and vulgar'. The Palace still exists but another remarkable hotel, the Empire, is only a memory. The Empire was one of the largest in Britain, built in 1906 on a site now occupied by a block of flats for the elderly beyond The Park, below the woods on Corbar Hill. By 1914 its last guests had gone and Canadian troops moved in but when they departed five years later the building was so badly damaged that it was left to decay. It was commandeered again by the War Office in 1939 and when vacated again was taken over by squatters. By the early sixties the Empire was virtually a ruin and eventually was demolished – having served the purpose for which it was built for only eight years!

The town has gained a new lease of life as a cultural centre. Its annual arts festival is nationally important, and the Pavilion and its gardens have been refurbished. The A6 trunk road has been re-routed to avoid the centre of the town, and the old Midland railway station has gone, though near its site is an expanding railway and transport museum.

Bathchairs are not seen near the baths any more, the thermal springs having declined, but Buxton remains a thriving town serving the needs of hordes of visitors and the semi-industrial quarry-based communities of the hills around it.

Chapel-en-le-Frith
Buxton's gain was Chapel's loss when the A6 trunk road was diverted northwards through Fairfield and Dove Holes. Travellers using Chapel's main street have seen a drab stone-built town with shops which, through no fault of their owners, have some of the dirtiest windows in the country. With the opening of the new Chapel-Whaley Bridge bypass, all that is changed.

'Chapel-en-le-Frith' denotes a chapel built in a clearing in the widely scattered King's Forest of the High Peak which in Norman times covered most of north-west Derbyshire and neighbouring counties. It was built on a knoll by foresters in 1225 and dedicated to St Thomas Becket but was replaced a century later by a more substantial building. In 1648 1,500 Scottish soldiers were imprisoned here by the Parliamentarians and were so overcrowded that after sixteen days here forty-four of them were dead; more perished on the forced march west into Cheshire. The church we see today near the delightful market-place is mainly from the rebuilding of 1733.

Few other old buildings survive in the town, which is surprising considering that it rose to become 'the Capital of the Peak', having taken on administrative and judicial functions by the end of the nineteenth century. Along the Chinley road, though, stands one of the world's largest brake-lining factories. Don't look for any particular geographical reasons for this; its location here is due to the chance factor that Herbert Frood lived at Combs close by. He was an engineer with an inventive mind and from 1897 experimented with various friction materials in his garden shed, making brake blocks for carts and traps before moving on to motor vehicles. His was a timely invention, and his company, Ferodo, is successful still.

Railway viaduct, Chapel Milton

A short distance beyond these works the Chinley road passes under one of the most magnificent monuments to the age of industry in Britain. The curving double stone viaduct of the former Midland Railway soars at over a hundred feet above the houses and seventeenth-century chapel here at Chapel Milton but is now used only by mineral and occasional excursion trains.

Glossop

With Buxton, this is the only truly Peak District town to have had
the status of a full borough. Glossop attained this distinction in
1866, over fifty years before Buxton. The settlement developed at
the western foot of the highest ground of Peakland as part of the
monastic estates of the abbey of Basingwerk, in north-east Wales.
The village got its market charter by 1290 but in succeeding
centuries declined in importance.

Old Glossop is the lovely, gritstone part of the town east of the
present centre where stand many fine examples of seventeenth-
century domestic architecture. Here is the parish church of All
Saints, of medieval origin but much added to.

Most people miss Old Glossop and its deserted market square;
many also drive through the town centre without realizing what a
good example it is of a new town of the early nineteenth century. It
was the brainchild of the lord of the manor, Bernard Edward
Howard, who became the twelfth Duke of Norfolk in 1816.
Assisted by a few aspirant industrialists, he established a model
Victorian settlement called Howard Town (New Glossop) complete with attractive square and finely proportioned town hall
(1838). The Hurst Reservoir was constructed in 1837 below the
Snake road to supply the growing number of cottonmills, and a
branch railway brought trains right into the town from the
Sheffield–Manchester line in Longdendale.

Cottages, Old Glossop

Glossop prospered. By the late nineteenth century its mighty mills were producing huge quantities of cheap fabrics for overseas markets, turned out by more than 800,000 spindles and 14,000 looms. All that, of course, has ended and most of the mills are no more, but the town – Howard Town and Old Glossop – remains attractively below those western hills. It has few pretensions, just a working countenance that knocks spots off the better-known, sugary tourist traps.

Leek

Leek is typical of several ancient boroughs at the very edge of the Peak District, within sight of the hills but not quite of them. The long hill road from Buxton comes down off Axe Edge and Ramshaw Rocks to enter the lowlands at Leek.

The town stands above a large meander of the River Churnet. It is red sandstone country; the parish church has a very ancient foundation (dedicated unusually to Edward the Confessor), and the present attractive building is more than 600 years old.

After gaining borough status in 1214, Leek became a thriving market centre ahead of Congleton and Macclesfield. Textile-manufacture has long been associated with this place, brought to the public notice a century ago when a group of townswomen took a year to make a copy of the Bayeux Tapestry (now in Reading Museum). The grassy lowlands and south Pennine foothills surrounding the town are an important dairying district and gave rise to the making of dairy products here – Adams Butter lorries were a common sight on Peak District roads, their product 'spreading everywhere'.

The town sits compactly on a mound, with the River Churnet curving round it to the west. There is much red brick in evidence, and tall textile mills and good views over pastoral country. The dark profiles of western Peakland lie as a far rampart to the east.

Macclesfield

Of all towns on the Peak District fringe, none sits closer to the foot of the hills than Macclesfield, just where the steep ground of Eddisbury and Blakelow drops to the very edge of the Cheshire Plain. And the best way to come to the town is from the east, down the road from Buxton and the high country with glimpses out across the plain. Then the grand, straight run down into Macclesfield, as good an entry into a town as any described here – but the promise does not hold, for at the bottom of the hill the town shows its seamier side. It is a nondescript perimeter to the

still-attractive town centre – the deteriorating townscape near the
railway station has caused a lot of local anguish.

The town became a free borough from Edward I in 1261, not
long after Leek. In the middle of the fifteenth century the Duke of
Buckingham lived here, in his castle perched upon a mound to the
south of the parish church. It was, apparently, more of a castellated mansion than a proper fortress. By 1585 it was described as
'a huge place all of stone . . . now gone to decay'.

The parish church stands in as commanding a position as any
in England, atop a bluff at the edge of the market-place. The best
way to appreciate this dramatic site is from the east, near the
railway station, for then we look up the full height of the bluff to
the dark stone church and the 108 steps that climb up to the
market-place beside it. Charles Tunnicliffe's painting *The Cattle
Market* shows this view about 1930, when the market was still held
down here near the station. Luckily this painting now hangs in the
town's West Park Museum.

Though textiles had been made here since the fourteenth
century, the first silkmill came into operation only in 1743.
Macclesfield became one of the most important silk-
manufacturing towns in the country, and other textile mills,
bleachworks and dyehouses added to the general prosperity in
Georgian times. Evidence of this is still obvious in the interesting
heart of the town: the good Georgian buildings of dark bricks in
Jordangate, King Edward Street and the market-place. Dominating the latter is the imposing town hall of 1824, built when the
town was enjoying its greatest industrial success, with seventy
factories recorded in operation.

At this time the Royal Independent stage-coach left the Pack
Horse in Jordangate every evening at nine, bound for London via
Leek, Ashbourne and Derby. Another coach left at 3.00 p.m. for
Manchester. Macclesfield had become an important town. Its
trade was not based entirely on textiles; there were, for instance,
no fewer than eight Kerridge stone-dealers with yards in the town
in the early nineteenth century.

A last word concerns an almost forgotten son of Macclesfield.
William Buckley was born here in the eighteenth century and
became a soldier. At Gibraltar he mutinied with fellow troops and
attempted to kill his commanding officer, the future father of
Queen Victoria. If Buckley had been more successful, we would
not have had a Victorian age! He was transported to Australia for
his trouble but escaped and established himself as chief of a tribe
of Aborigines. After living with his new friends for thirty-two

years, he returned to civilization near the coast, was pardoned and lived to be seventy-six years old.

Matlock

When Ruskin came here, the Derwent ran through a limestone dale that was relatively unspoilt, so his admonition to 'think of what this little piece of mid-England has brought into so narrow a compass of all that should be most precious to you' was correct, quite in order. At the beginning of this century J. B. Firth wrote that he believed Ruskin's 'indignation would rise at every step' at the damage wrought by man on this valley. And what would Firth, let alone Ruskin, make of the dale now?

Matlock was in existence at the Domesday Survey, its name probably originating as 'the oak where the moot was held', but not the place we think of now – only the little original settlement clustered insignificantly near the parish church at the foot of the slope below Riber Hill.

The Heights of Abraham is the name given to the steep and wooded ground that rises directly above Matlock Bath on its western side. It takes its name from local enthusiasm for Wolfe's victory at Quebec. Travellers on the A6 between Matlock Bath and Matlock Bridge may notice cables slanting across the dale high overhead. These carry the new cable cars up to the top of the Heights of Abraham, a popular attraction in summer which takes much of the effort out of getting onto high ground.

One of the most popular attractions with early visitors was Matlock Bath's petrifying well, which still exists. Objects left to be dripped on are slowly coated with a deposit of calcium carbonate, apparently turned to stone by the magic of the spa waters.

Then the crossing-point of the Derwent developed as Matlock Bridge, an important meeting-place of turnpike roads in a lead-mining district. Then the spring waters in the limestone gorge downstream of the village began to attract visitors, and Matlock Bath came into being in the shadowed and chilly rift. The place was popular with the wealthy and took on the air of a spa, with walks in the steep woods above the Derwent and conducted tours of the several caverns. With the coming of the railway in 1849, Matlock Bath began to attract hordes of day-trippers, and the number of 'health-seekers of the highest class' fell away. The advent of motor transport hastened the trend so that the place is now somewhere to avoid like the plague – unless the goal is pink candyfloss, deafening disco music and rowdy weekend crowds.

Last to develop was Matlock Bank, the steep ground to the east of the Derwent, above Matlock Bridge. John Smedley is the father of Matlock Bank, a wealthy textile-mill owner who set about creating a hydropathic health spa. He built Smedley's Hydro high on the slope in 1853, and many more such establishments sprang up later. This face of the town has completely disappeared – Smedley's Hydro is now the headquarters of Derbyshire County Council. Matlock Bank presents a rather sad countenance now, its steep and draughty streets and grey stone houses a reminder of a fairly short and quite vanished period in the town's evolution.

Across the valley, atop Riber Hill, stands the grim, toy fortress silhouette of Smedley's Riber Castle (1862–8) built as the great man's home but defeated by lack of water at this 850-foot elevation. It now houses a zoo for European fauna.

Firth went on to detail his disgust, concluding that, 'The debasing influence of the day tripper is everywhere visible in Matlock.' Firth and Ruskin would be even more disappointed and disgusted by the present town but their likely apoplexy could not be treated locally, for all the hydropathic establishments have long since disappeared.

Penistone

The ancient Cut Gate track still traverses the high watershed between Derwent Dale and the valley of the Porter or Little Don. Its surface might be much eroded but its line is just as it was when it was the packhorse way for the farmers of the Hope Valley, Woodlands and Derwent Dale going to and from Penistone market.

This South Yorkshire town is one of the least pretentious of those described here. Standing at about 750 feet above sea-level in the upper valley of the Don, it has a dark countenance for its gritstone buildings have been much blackened by steam trains and twentieth-century industry. Its heart is typical of smaller towns on the eastern Pennine slopes: some nice cottages and larger houses in that useful local stone.

The thirteenth-century parish church of St John the Baptist stands at the centre of the little town, its tall Perpendicular tower (rebuilt about 1500) the most conspicuous architectural feature for miles around. The dark trees of the churchyard overshadow the graves of the Wordsworths, long-time residents here and relatives of the poet.

Penistone railway viaduct and parish church from the north-east

The town deserves a careful inspection. There are the Cloth Hall and Shambles of 1768, near the church, and the early Victorian townhouse in the main street with its three storeys almost all of glass – not the easiest dwelling to keep warm in winter. And what of Penistone's notorious climate? It all started with a Sheffield journalist's comment in 1882 that anyone who had been to the town would be fully prepared for life at the North Pole. Yes, Penistone stands on a north-facing slope above 700 feet but it is certainly no more inhospitable than, say, Buxton and is to some extent sheltered by the higher ground to the west. A healthy sort of place to live in.

At the southern edge of town is Cubley Garden Village, good-looking, semi-detached houses rather like coastguard houses and built here after the Great War for the local steel-workers, now rather dilapidated and built between, with poorly designed dwellings and being surrounded by new houses of altogether different and inferior style.

Seen from the high ground across the Don Valley, say from near Hoyland Swaine, the town is dominated by the grand stone viaduct built in 1885 to carry the branch railway to Huddersfield but, unbelievably, a new estate of houses has been allowed to be built almost under it, to the west, so removing some of the drama of this fine Victorian structure.

Penistone became an important railway town when the early trans-Pennine Woodhead route of the Sheffield, Ashton-under-

Lyne and Manchester Railway (opened 1845) passed through, and later branches to Huddersfield and Barnsley made it a busy junction. Two historic railway disasters here were separated by less than six months.

On a July day in 1884 the 12.40 p.m. Manchester–King's Cross express was coming down from Woodhead Tunnel hauled by a 423-class engine when a crank axle broke, snapping the coupling between the tender and first carriage. With the Smith's simple vacuum system in use, all braking was immediately lost. The locomotive and tender remained on the embankment but the rest of the train shot down the slope to pile up on the road at Bullhouse Bridge. Twenty-four lives were lost and sixty people were injured.

On New Year's Day 1885 a Manchester-bound excursion train was approaching Penistone station when a de-railed goods waggon on a Sheffield-bound freight train ripped out the sides of several carriages. Six passengers were killed.

The formerly busy Woodhead line was electrified in 1954, when the new tunnel was opened to traffic; in 1970 passenger services were withdrawn, and in July 1981 the route was finally closed to all traffic. The busy inter-city rail route has gone, and though at the time of writing trains still climb the Don Valley to Penistone and go on over the long viaduct to Huddersfield, even this branch is threatened with closure.

The ancient Penistone breed of horned sheep almost vanished, too, but that has seen a slight rise in its fortunes of late and is being preserved on several farms in the district, virtually the same as the White-faced Woodland breed of the Hope Woodlands.

Saddleworth
Until Local Government re-organization in 1974 this was one of those anomalous places which was part of Yorkshire's West Riding but stood in the narrow confines of the Tame Valley and topographically looked west. Despite local objections at the time, Saddleworth became part of Greater Manchester after re-organization.

One of the best places to get a proper perspective of this urban district formed of several distinct villages is from high on Dick Hill, that lofty spur between the Greenfield and Tame Valleys where stands Saddleworth's conspicuous Great War memorial which must be one of the best situated in the country.

A long and straggling conglomeration of stone and brick houses, factories and shops fills the narrow floor of the dale, winding northwards towards Diggle, where the gritstone moors frown down. The name Saddleworth includes the individual villages of Greenfield, Uppermill, Dobcross and others. Sheep-farming was the main occupation, of course, with spinning and weaving a cottage-based industry until factories spread up the valley in the early nineteenth century. From that time textile-manufacture and the allied dyestuffs industry have employed most of the population.

There has, of course, been a recent drastic retraction in employ-ment in Saddleworth's mills. Some have closed, others are used for new industries. The Huddersfield Narrow Canal was aban-doned in 1944 but the railway between Manchester and Leeds still winds along the side of the valley before vanishing into Standedge Tunnel at Diggle. Tourism has come to the Tame Valley; there is a good museum at Uppermill, in a former cottonmill, and every Whitsuntide there is the nationally famous brass band contest – 'Hail, Smiling Morn' and that sort of thing.

Anyone exploring this drawn-out urban area will notice the number of long rows of mullioned windows still lighting the upper floors of many older houses, a reminder of the days when most householders had a loom and weaving was the mainstay of a civilized cottage economy under the high hills.

Wirksworth
This ancient township – literally 'enclosure of Weorc or Wyrc' – stands virtually at the centre of Derbyshire but at the south-eastern edge of the Peak District, about two miles from the nearest point of the National Park boundary. It is one of the oldest commercial centres of the South Pennines and was the centre of the English lead mining industry.

Pevsner reminds us that Wirksworth is the place where the Barmote Courts are held, in the rebuilt (1814) Moot Hall in Chapel Lane. Lead-mining was going on here in Roman, then Saxon, times but has virtually vanished from the Peak District; limestone quarrying has taken its place, and there are some impressive quarries at Middleton to the north-west of the town.

Wirksworth is a good example of a nucleated settlement with a central market-place. The parish church of St Mary is one of the most interesting in Peakland and its fringes, dating from 1272 when the first vicar was appointed. There was a church here in Saxon times, subordinate to Repton Abbey, but that has been completely replaced by the 'new' building. The church is not particularly conspicuous from the town centre, but once the visitor has seen it, he will not mistake it for any other because of the unusual spire. The tower's lower part dates from the thirteenth century, its upper half is early fourteenth century, and sitting atop this is the comical 'spike' or mini-spire. Though eccentric at first glance, this feature works quite well and cannot be mistaken for any other in the area.

The annual Whitsuntide well dressing was initiated in 1827 as an expression of thanks to landowners who had allowed the first tap water to be brought to the town in wooden pipes over their land.

There are memorials inside to the important Gells of nearby Hopton and the Hurts of Alderwasley Hall. (The popular Victorian artist Louis Bosworth Hurt (1865–1929), best known for his paintings of Highland cattle in grand Highland landscapes, was one of this family.) The church had an interesting curate in the late eighteenth century in the Reverend Abraham Bennett FRS, author of *New Experiments on Electricity*.

Wirksworth is the 'Snowfield' of George Eliot's *Adam Bede*: a cottage beside Derby Road was the home of 'Dinah Morris's' prototype, and the novelist's uncle Samuel Evans was manager of the Haarlem Tape Works which still stand beside the road, a mile south of the town centre.

From the slanting market-place the town spreads in all directions and repays a careful exploration. There are some lovely old buildings, many now restored as part of a comprehensive civic scheme. No single structure is outstanding but the site of the town centre is attractive, and the whole ensemble is the memorable thing about Wirksworth. After years of quiet neglect it is being put tastefully in order and serves as a focal point for a large rural district.

Three Rivers' Journey

On a wet January day I walked with a companion northwards out of Hartington, by the oval duckpond and Moat Hall and along the narrowing lane just above the alder-lined Dove. The river was brimming to its banks after days of rain. The straight valley ahead was dismal indeed, grey mist cutting off the hilltops to make them look higher than their rather modest 1,200 feet.

This part of the Dove's valley is not well known; I dare say it is one of the least frequented parts of the lower Peak District – in sharp contrast to the 'honeypot' Dovedale proper between Thorpe and Milldale. To this latter limestone gorge come thousands of visitors every fine week-end, so that it has become little more than a public park with such wear-and-tear on its riverside path that steps have had to be taken to prevent serious erosion. Steps and handrails may do the trick but all sense of discovering wild nature has been destroyed as one tries to make progress through the picnic parties near the stepping-stones below Thorpe Cloud on a hot Sunday afternoon, or queue to make progress further up the dale.

The early travellers who admired this gorge of the Dove, including Byron and Gilpin, would see it in a more open state than now for the all-enveloping ashwoods which rather hide the classic rock spires and small cliffs above the river had not grown up. It has been calculated that most of these trees are only a century and a half old; before that time the gorge would be more open, its rock architecture far more conspicuous. These modern woods do have a bonus in the autumn, though, when the dale is turned momentarily to liquid gold.

Those lucky, earlier visitors saw Dovedale at its best and there are some flowery descriptions in early topographical works. Bemroses' *Illustrated Guide to Derbyshire* refers to the narrowest part as 'Dovedale Straits', a 'chasm so narrow that, when by heavy rains the stream is swollen, the passage through it becomes impracticable'.

In July 1761 Dean Langton of Clogher was staying with the Cokes at Longford Hall and joined a party to Dovedale. They took refreshment near Reynard's Cave and prepared to return via Tissington. Langton took a young lady of the party, Miss La Roche, on horseback up the steep hillside towards the village but took the wrong path. When he found it becoming too steep, he tried to turn the horse round but it was 'overpowered by the burden imposed upon him and fell backwards down the hill'. The horse was only slightly hurt but Dean Langton was thrown to the bottom of the slope and so badly hurt that he died a few days later. Miss La Roche had her fall broken when her hair became entangled in a thorn tree, and she escaped with 'severe contusions though for two days she continued insensible'.

Reynard's Cave (or Hall) near the place where the accident occurred seems to have been a popular spot from the earliest days. A century and more ago a traveller reported, 'The broken glass, orange peel, and other fragmentary remains we find scattered about, are so many evidences which tell of frolic, feast and fun.' Litter is not such a new problem in Dovedale as we might think.

Early topographers did not always get their facts right – one writer described Reynard's Cave as a 'cavernous chamber or opening, formed by the shrinking of the strata during the cooling of the great limestone bubble'. The cave is, in fact, what is left of a river-worn hollow; the Dove continued to cut down and reached its present depth with the former river feature abandoned high above and guarded by the impressive arch which we must climb through to reach the cave-mouth. Likewise, the famous limestone towers poking through the tree-tops are probably all that is left of cavern walls or very hard cores of limestone.

The Dove is a trout stream *par excellence* and has been ever since the immortal Charles Cotton and Izaak Walton plied their sport here. Fishing is strictly private in the gorge and for miles up-stream, beyond Milldale, up Wolfscote Dale (not 'wolf' but 'Wulfstan's cottage') and Beresford Dale to Hartington and beyond. Beresford Dale is only short, lovely and tree-shaded with its still, dark Pike Pool and towering spike of fern-covered lime-stone. Nearby is the easily missed Fishing House built by Cotton in 1674, where the two anglers spent many hours and developed the art of angling. Beresford Hall stood not far away, up on the western (Staffordshire) slope above the river. It was Cotton's home but was demolished about 1860 after the wealthy Anglo-Catholic Alexander Beresford Hope inherited it. All that remains today, besides the Fishing House by the river, is the pair of

Hollinsclough hamlet in the Upper Dove Valley

important-looking gateposts on the Hartington-Hulme End road.

North of Beresford Dale the valley broadens; there are fewer trees, and the path crosses stone-walled pastures to Hartington. Here is one of Peakland's most aesthetically pleasing and popular villages, that popularity now rather spoiling its real appeal. There are more craftshops and cafés than ordinary shops, a common enough trend in 'honeypot' areas these days.

The most obvious interesting building is the classical town hall of 1836 with its rusticated arches partly hiding the shop within. Lying back, up the slope, is the parish church of St Giles, partly thirteenth-century and containing a small Saxon stone in the north transept wall. In the tower are three seventeenth-century bells, and the clock was built in 1781 to replace an earlier one, using the oldest bell (cast in 1636) to proclaim the hours. A glass case on a bracket in the south transept once contained an armour gauntlet originally thought to have been used at Agincourt, but in the mid 1950s an authority considered it to have been made about 1620. It was passed down in the Bateman family and was finally stolen from this glass case in May 1983.

The Batemans are worth more than a mention. They came first to Hartington in the fifteenth century and climbed the social ladder so that by 1806 they had achieved a baronetcy. Two centuries earlier they had built delightful Hartington Hall, above the village on the lane to Biggin and Heathcote. It is a typical Derbyshire yeoman's house with three gables and mullioned windows; restored early this century, it is now a youth hostel.

All this brings us back to that wet January day as we walked northwards out of the village, along the narrow lane above the alder-lined Dove by Banktop Farm. Ahead is that virtually unknown part of the valley, empty and quiet and all the better for it. The lane eventually swings back to climb the steep slope eastwards, crossing the plateau near Mosey Low before reaching the Ashbourne-Buxton highway south of Flagg Moor. At this point, where the lane swings back up the slope above the Dove, is Pilsbury. Two large farms with tall, grey houses looking across the valley are protected by great deciduous trees; there are the impedimenta of generations of farming strewn about, which adds to the forgotten nature of the place. Just beyond, above the river, stands enigmatic Pilsbury Castle. No one has excavated the site, but we can conjecture that this was an Iron Age fortress which was the focal settlement for all the upper Dove Valley. Later the Normans used Pilsbury as the site of a castle founded about 1100 to command hostile country. Maybe the inhabitants of this marginal area moved away to more fertile lowland, leaving one of the many 'wastes' recorded so often by the Domesday surveyors. Whatever happened here, Pilsbury with its grassy ramparts is an enchanting place, all the more so for its total neglect over several centuries.

Just across the river, on the Staffordshire slope, stands seventeenth-century Broadmeadow Hall with its tall gables ornamented with ball finials. It has mullioned windows on three floors, the lower two with transoms. For many years this grand house lay empty because the farmer went to live at Sheen, over the hill, and none of his sons was married, so it was used as a store. Now, though, a son has taken a wife, and Broadmeadow Hall is inhabited again.

Further up this straight section of the valley the road to Longnor crosses the river. Here, ranged up the Derbyshire slope, is Crowdecote, pretty cottages tumbled together on the hillside where the road twists this way and that. A spring of clear water caused Crowdecote to develop here as 'Cruda's cottage'. The quiet days – when pigs grunted in their sties and multi-coloured poultry scratched on the gravel road, and straw was strewn out of steep yards – have long since gone; like so many backwater settlements, it has been tidied up and lost its soul in the process.

Upper Manifold Valley with Chrome Hill

From Crowdecote the unique hills of the upper Dove are seen to advantage. These are the shapeliest little eminences of the Peak District – Chrome Hill and Parkhouse Hill – which are the remnants of coral reefs every bit as impressive as Australia's Great Barrier Reef, almost detached from the mass of limestone behind by the deepening of inter-reef channels. Later sandstones and shales were deposited in these canyons so that these sharp peaks now stand almost surrounded by the later shales which are the harbinger of the darker countryside of the uppermost Dove. Caves in these reefs and neighbouring limestone, like Fox Hole on High Wheeldon Hill and Dowel between Chrome and Parkhouse, were inhabited by the earliest settlers. Dowel Cave has given up its store of prehistoric relics through the years, including hundreds of bones of woodland and water birds, oxen, bats and small rodents.

The Dove comes down from its source on the side of Axe Edge to reach this fringe of the limestone plateau. Upstream of these conspicuous reef knolls of Chrome and Parkhouse we are in quite different country: attractive brown gritstone upland but with an impoverished sort of countenance. This is by no means affluent agricultural territory – the soil and the climate have seen to that.

Just across the speeding Dove from Chrome Hill stands delightful Hollinsclough hamlet at a junction of minor roads, beneath old trees. There is a simple chapel, grand stone cottages and the church with unusual obelisk-topped gables. It was built in 1840 and is semi-detached to a house.

The lane to the west climbs steeply out of Hollinsclough to leave the river swirling below in its secret upper dale where an ancient bridleway crosses on a narrow packhorse bridge at the place made famous in the motorcycle world as a difficult observed section in trials competitions. The river continues to form the boundary between Derbyshire and Staffordshire right up to its source; the two counties face each other across the narrowing valley where isolated hill farms stand looking blankly out across the wild, gritstone landscape. It is little wonder that the Domesday surveyors referred to much of this western upland as 'waste'; at that time it seems that the poverty-stricken smallholders had moved *en masse* to better, lowland districts and left this dark country 'totally desolate'. It looks desolate in poor weather even today, and a new wave of migration has taken place in recent years. Many of the bleakly situated farms on the side of Axe Edge and Brand Top, for instance, are either abandoned or commuters' dwellings or even 'second homes'.

The Dove has its source at a spring called Dove Head, just below the Buxton-Leek road (A53). The stone slab on top of the trough where the spring runs has the interlocked initials of Izaak Walton and Charles Cotton carved on it. The two illustrious anglers may have followed their favourite river to its lofty source but were certainly not responsible for these romantic graffiti. They died in 1683 and 1687 respectively, and this carving was done much later. A severe frost in 1903 cracked the stone but did not damage the initials.

Less than a mile to the south of Dove Head stands Flash Head, near the highest village in Peakland. Beyond that, to the west, is the country described in the next chapter. Here, though, the Manifold rises, near Flash Head, that other major river of this south-western quarter of the district. In some ways it is more important than the Dove, draining a larger, more open basin. It certainly has a character of its own and for several miles drains the wild gritstone hills before crossing onto limestone territory at Hulme End.

High in its infant hills are lovely, secret bowers, unfrequented by the hordes. There are Dun Cow Grove, Thick Withens and Hardings Booth – forgotten places under broad, western skies with the darkling tops of the Staffordshire moorlands as guardians.

A little lower downstream the Manifold comes within less than a mile of the Dove before turning southwards. Here the two rivers are separated only by a narrow ridge of sandstone, and upon the Manifold side of this stands Longnor, called by Henry Thorold 'a miniature market town in farthermost, northernmost Stafford-shire' – an apt description. Longnor stands better, to my mind, than Hartington because it lies on a slope with its square and Victorian market hall. The latter was put up in 1873, at a time when the settlement's aspirations were still optimistic. It had grown as the urban centre for the expanding farmlands of the high moors to the west. The squatters came to seek their fortunes on these unforgiving wastes; a market was held in the little square, and the old church was rebuilt in 1780 (its Classical Georgian exterior proclaims its date).

With the coming of turnpike roads, Longnor became quite an important crossroads, and its several inns thrived. It is not difficult to imagine a stage-coach pulled up outside the Crewe and Harper Arms, its horses being changed, its passengers refreshing themselves within. But Longnor never saw a railway and slowly faded away. It remains largely unspoilt to this day, looking out over the green fields of the Manifold to clouds piled above the western gritstone heights.

Three miles down that narrow ridge between Dove and Manifold is another little place left alone by time. Sheen Hill rises to 1,247 feet, and leafy Sheen stands just below. A glance at the map might give the idea of a bleak, wind-blasted village of the uplands but there are plenty of planted trees about the place, a legacy from the days of Alexander Beresford Hope in the middle of the last century.

As we come down the lane from Longnor and the side of Sheen Hill, the first thing we notice is a tall, narrow stone building in a field, beginning to tumble down. It is said to be a remnant of the dwellings which once stood here, on the village's northern fringe. Lower down are the trees and fine old farms and the remarkable church of 1852 by Butterfield, replacing an older one. In the graveyard is a remarkable memorial to several Critchlows who died in the middle of the nineteenth century, all within a short time of one another as victims of a local 'plague' thought to have been caused by infection in a village well – natural spring water was not always what we might think it was, looking back through rose-tinted spectacles from the late twentieth century. I have never seen a more claustrophobic tomb than this one in Sheen graveyard, wrapped about with ornate cast iron, offering no hope of escape to the occupants.

Near the church are the school and Butterfield's impressive vicarage, looking more like the manor house. It is roofed with the dark Staffordshire tiles which keep out the rain on so many buildings in this part of England. This tree-girt part of Sheen has a cosy, old-world feel but there are reminders of harder times. In a field to the north-west of Sheen Hill stands Froom Barn, which during the last century lodged an itinerant farmworker helping with the harvest. His lonely demise was discovered only when a white cow in a stall in the barn was found with blood splashes on her back. Poor Froom had taken his own life in the loft above.

The lane through the village goes southwards for a mile and a half to the main road at Hulme End. Here are a fine bridge over the Manifold and a hotel, and just beyond, to the west, the site of the terminus of the delightfully conceived Leek and Manifold Valley Light Railway. If one was looking for a suitable route for a tourist railway nowadays, it would be hard to find a better one than this, but in 1904, when this railway was opened, tourism was only part of its *raison d'être*. Its other function was to transport coal and other bulky raw materials to outlying settlements and to serve the creamery at Ecton, a mile south of Hulme End.

The railway had a gauge of two feet six inches and left the standard gauge North Staffordshire line at Waterhouses on the Ashbourne–Leek road (A523). Progress was made northwards in this unpromising railway countryside of steep valleys and high hills by following the banks of the tributary River Hamps downstream to its confluence with the Manifold, then keeping close to the sharp meanderings of the latter past Ecton to Hulme End.

Two steam locomotives were built to an Indian design, so accurately that they carried large headlamps that were quite superfluous. The passengers in those quiet, far-off days may well have imagined they were traversing the Indian hills, for the yellow-painted carriages had verandahs. The only hindrances seem to have been straying cattle. What a comfortable sight it must have been to espy from some high, green hilltop the little train sending up its dark trail of smoke and steam from the wooded riverside below. What hectic dashes to the nearest station some rambling parties must have made as the last train of the day approached through the trees. The line, though, did not pay its way, especially after the closure of Ecton creamery in 1933, and was closed in 1934. The rails were carted away, and we might never have known of its existence if its course had not been turned into a footpath (a pioneer semi-long-distance path). There are one or two railway relics remaining – modest buildings, a tiny tunnel – but, to quote Henry Thorold, the railway 'arrived too late, and left too early'. Yes, it certainly would enjoy a boom today.

Rather more than a mile to the south-west of Hulme End stands Warslow, a rather large village at almost 1,000 feet. At the eastern foot of those dark Staffordshire moorlands. It is a former estate village of the Harpur-Crewes of Calke Abbey, away in the softer south Derbyshire countryside. Warslow Hall is a Georgian building which served the family as a shooting lodge, a fine house sheltered by a high wall and mature trees aloof from the village by the Longnor road.

As you approach Warslow these days, the most conspicuous building is the modern secondary school, serving a wide area of south-western Peakland's hills and valleys. In bad weather Warslow is a welcome little haven at the edge of those expansive, brown moors that swell from Morridge to Axe Edge.

The four-mile-long Warslow Brook is one of the least-known streams of all, wandering eastwards from the top of these Staffordshire moorlands, at 1,603 feet Merryton Low, to join the Manifold near Warslow. In it are isolated farms, stone cottages and small, hidden woods. When the low, late summer sun sinks beyond the high ground, great shadows punctuate this quiet, unassuming valley. Lower Elkstone is a scattering of country homes dotted along the lane which winds towards those frowning hills. Less than a mile beyond, across Warslow Brook, stands Upper Elkstone with its 200-year-old church with lovely, round-headed sash windows – all very authentic Georgian and in fine condition.

This tributary joins the Manifold opposite the massive bulk of Ecton Hill (1,212 feet), one of the several uplands seen on the near horizon when looking south from the neighbourhood of Sheen. Having traversed its broad, upper valley, the Manifold now forces its way off the impervious shales and gritstones and into limestone country. It does this by a tight and sinuous route immediately west of Ecton Hill, almost a gorge but without the many bare limestone rock features of the neighbouring Dove. Tiny Ecton hamlet lies close by the river, opposite Warslow, and it is now hard to imagine it as the site of great industrial activity in earlier times. Copper ores were discovered and first mined here in the mid seventeenth century, and the introduction of gunpowder some time later quickly increased the industrial output – indeed, Ecton is claimed to have been one of the first sites in the country where gunpowder was utilized.

The fifth Duke of Devonshire owned most of the mineral rights at Ecton, and it is generally accepted that the profits from these copper workings paid for the construction of his Crescent at Buxton. Between 1776 and 1817 nearly 54,000 tons of copper ore were extracted, bringing a profit of about £6,000 per annum. About fifty miners were employed, and fifty women equipped with hammers broke it up on the surface. One of these mines – the Deep Ecton at the northern end of Ecton Hill – was nearly 1,400 feet deep, one of the deepest in Europe. Most work stopped here between 1880 and 1900 but so impervious were the surrounding limestones that the workings took seven years to flood. Many of them are now under water.

A couple of miles to the south-west of Ecton under its broad, round hill stands one of the nicest upland villages of all. Set about the thousand-foot contour, Butterton has plenty of trees and a lofty spire of 1879 on the parish church, stone houses and cottages, a steep street or two and the little Hoo Brook in its sheltered dell – all very attractive; it is often hard to believe one is so high, and so near the western moors.

Little more than a mile to the south-east of Butterton stands a similar Staffordshire hill village but much closer to the Manifold valley. Grindon likewise lies at the thousand-foot level with a 400-foot slope down to the winding river. To use the light railway all those years ago, residents and visitors had to go up and down that steep gradient to the station called 'Weags Bridge for Grindon'. My memory is of Grindon's slender spire rising distantly as seen in summer heat from the vicinity of Thor's Cave, a sleeping village in lonely country; was it, one wondered from afar, still inhabited? When you pull up one of the lanes to Grindon, you will find a living place dominated by that sharp spire on the church of 1848. There are other attractive buildings here, typical humble, stone dwellings of upland Staffordshire.

There are two gems. As you come up that steep lane from Weags Bridge, there is a totally unspoilt farm building on the right, a little cowshed-cum-barn with an old growth of ivy upon it, and an ancient oak beam doing service as a lintel on the side wall, all very rustic and as unassuming as the cattle who look out over the stable door on winter days. Further on, look towards the church at a fork in the lane and see the excellent placing of a row of council houses, stepped up the slope and leading the eye towards that slender spire; all modern planning isn't bad after all!

Thor's Cave is the great natural sight of the Manifold, a magnificent opening in a limestone crag high on the eastern slope of the valley. The steep ascent to the entrance gives the impression of the approach to a cathedral door, wide open and shadowy within. The first serious archaeologists were local men – Thomas Bateman (the family already mentioned as resident at Hartington) and Samuel Carrington, schoolmaster, of Wetton – and they discovered Samian pottery, iron objects and a Roman coin. In the second and third centuries this and adjacent caves seem to have been inhabited by shepherds, even miners and the temporary homeless. After Carrington's rather rough treatment of the excavated material here in 1864, the great geologist W. Boyd Dawkins came a decade later, reported in his *Cave Hunting* of 1874 (reprinted in 1974).

Then in 1935 the Reverend G. H. Wilson discovered a small-mouthed cave behind an elder bush only a short distance from Thor's Cave. It contains a complicated system of passages, and herein were discovered (between 1935 and 1952) a rich store of lion, hyaena, wolf, hippopotamus and other animal bones of inter-glacial times. They were identified by the eminent geologist and palaeontologist Dr J. W. Jackson who lived at Buxton to such a great age. At the deepest level of deposits a fragment of reindeer

Manifold Valley with Thor's Cave

bone shaped to a point by some late Palaeolithic man was discovered, the oldest artefact discovered here. At an even deeper level were discovered worked flints and charcoal – maybe all we shall ever know of nomadic people warming themselves here as the last glaciers melted. Elderbush Cave is one of the most important archaeological sites in this part of England. Indeed, the Manifold is the most highly concentrated area for archaeological caves in the Peak District.

Another interesting cave is St Bertram's in the reef limestone of Beeston Tor, just above the Manifold's banks half a mile south of Thor's Cave. It is remarkable as the place where Wilson unearthed a cache of Saxon treasures earlier this century. He found forty-nine silver coins struck in the time of several ninth-century kings, a gold circlet, gold rings and silver brooches, all probably hidden here by monks to avoid their being stolen by Viking marauders. Though this cave used to have a door, it is now open for spelaeologists, a 600-foot-long system with muddy crawls suitable for beginners.

Up on the edge of the limestone plateau to the east lies Wetton, a typical village of the White Peak, open to the elements at the thousand-foot contour. Narrow lanes lead gently from Alstonefield to Wetton in contrast to those from Butterton and Grindon, which dip and twist across the Manifold Valley at fearful gradients. The medieval church was largely rebuilt in 1820 and contains the royal arms of George IV. But the village is more important historically than one might at first imagine: Carrington excavated the Borough Fields adjacent to Wetton between 1845 and 1852 and discovered an abandoned village. Neither he nor his friend Bateman could decide the age of the site, or why it was finally abandoned. It may be an Anglican settlement raided by Danes in the ninth century, or could have been a thriving village well into the Middle Ages and eventually wiped out by the infamous Black Death. Whatever really happened, the present village became the centre of population several centuries ago, a collection of stone cottages and farms surrounded by countless grey-white field walls under a broad sky.

If Thor's Cave is the most dramatic sight of the Manifold Valley, the nature of the river downstream of Wetton Mill is the most intriguing; it disappears from view for several miles unless there has been prolonged rainfall. Below the mill the river soaks underground, leaving only a few still pools. Through the years fruitless attempts have been made to block the leaks with cement and tar but no one has succeeded and the river hides away whenever there is a dry spell. It comes to the surface again in a group of at least eight resurgences near Ilam Hall. Dye tests have shown that water disappearing near Wetton Mill takes 20½ hours to cover the four miles, a vertical fall of about 150 feet. In summer it is a pleasant pastime to walk along the stony bed of the Manifold, avoiding the pools and luxuriant growths of butterbur.

Now we come to the major Manifold tributary, the River Hamps, which rises on the dark moorlands not far from the Warslow Brook and has a most remarkable course of a dozen miles to join the parent river opposite Beeston Tor.

Lonely farms dot the hill slopes of the upper Hamps valley, beef and sheep predominate, and few visitors ever seem to wander in this quiet country. Ancient Black Brook Farm, beside a tiny tributary, shelters in its secret hollow, brown stone walls and huge mauve slates on its roof. A brass tablet on the wall of Upper Elkstone's pretty church proclaims that the eighty-seven-year-old owner of Black Brook died in 1897; his farm realized £1,024, which went to the coffers of the Church Commissioners. What might the busy little farm fetch on the open market now?

The Hamps wanders on to Onecote (pronounced locally On-cut) beside the Warslow–Cheadle road. It is a scattered sort of village, rather spoilt by the speeding traffic. The church, though, lies back to the west and is nicer within than you would expect: the Venetian east window is a little Georgian gem, and the painted Commandments board of 1755 confronting you at the west end as you enter is warm with coloured Bible characters. Just to reinforce the former stability of the local inhabitants is a brass plate to a member of the Edge family, who farmed Acre Farm continuously from the eleventh to the nineteenth century.

A mile downstream is pretty Ford, a hamlet of working farms at a former ford on the Hamps and now crossed by a bridge. The semi-detached Georgian farmhouse near the bridge is a good example of the importance of correct and incorrect window styles. The right-hand house has perfectly proportioned panes with slender glazing bars but the left-hand one has modern, ill-proportioned window frames which spoil the effect of the entire building.

Beyond Ford the Hamps meanders southwards over the National Park boundary to Winkhill and on to Waterhouses alongside the busy Ashbourne–Leek highway (A523) where the Leek and Manifold Valley Light Railway joined the standard-gauge line to Leek. Here, where the river re-enters the National Park, a strange thing occurs. As with the Manifold near Wetton

Mill, the Hamps comes onto limestone and suddenly disappears underground through shack-holes. The river has been heading generally south-eastwards but here below Waterhouses it swerves due north to flow for 2½ miles in a ravine to join the Manifold at Beeston Tor. The light railway ran beside the river, its course now smooth for walking as it bends below steep woods, in and out of the shadows with the usually dry bed of the Hamps always close. But the big mystery here is that sudden change in direction near Waterhouses. What we see is a grand example of river-capture, but what initiated this turning to the north when natural drainage would be towards the south-east and the Dove below Ashbourne? Maybe several river-captures whose pattern is largely lost in the present topography, or blockage by ice. One day thorough fieldwork may come up with an answer.

Anyone walking or driving on the lanes above Waterfall or Grindon will not fail, in clear weather, to notice the great and offensive quarry at Cauldon a mile to the south of Waterhouses. A towering chimney spews thick smoke into the clear, upland air, a collection of buildings which emulate a distant prospect of Hong Kong, and wide open scars on Cauldon Low assault the eyes. This nastiness may stand outside the National Park but its stark affront on these swelling, green hills is insupportable.

Throwley Hall

Hidden away above a small tributary of the Hamps is one last village, a tiny place called Waterfall with a grey church dedicated to St John and St Bartholomew. Its Norman chancel arch has sunk to look lop-sided, its old oak chancel panelling is dark and its imposing churchyard gates look grand indeed. Below the church are the farms in the district called Back o' th' Brook, a real sun-trap at the foot of Waterfall Low. One farm where toy tractors are often parked at the laneside is called Under the Low – what a magic address – Under the Low, Back o' th' Brook, Waterfall, Staffordshire.

Lower down the Manifold Valley, a mile below its confluence with the Hamps near Beeston Tor, stand the evocative ruins of Throwley Hall. This was the seat of the Meverells but the male line petered out in 1626 and the last Meverell, Robert, lies in Ilam church. Now the mellow ruin sleeps adjacent to the still-busy farm of the same name. Just across the river to the east, at a similar altitude, stands Castern Hall; tucked away from the public gaze, it is an elegant eighteenth-century house built by the Hurts of Alderwasley, illustrious ironfounders at that time and now resident here again.

And so we come to Ilam, famous as the pretty place not far from the confluence of Manifold and Dove which Dr Samuel Johnson admired. Boswell extolled the views from Ilam Hall, the steep slopes and hanging woods and 'walks neatly formed'. The Saxons farmed the higher ground above the valley, and St Bertram's shrine stands within the ancient church. Jesse Watts Russell bought Ilam Hall early in the last century and had it re-modelled (unfortunately) by Shaw in 1821. Russell's efforts to ornament the dwellings of his humble workers can be seen in the village, and then, in 1855, Gilbert Scott was employed to rebuild the church and add the fine mausoleum which contains Chantrey's sensitive carved monument to Russell's father-in-law. What remains of the Hall serves as a youth hostel, focal point of an estate which finally passed to the National Trust in 1934.

A short walk upstream to Darfur Crags bring us to the main resurgences of the Manifold, probably eight in number, where the disappearing waters come finally to the surface – a phenomenon, incidentally, which Dr Johnson treated with some scepticism.

Ilam is a valley-bottom village, and a steep lane climbs due south for a mile from its bridge to the ridge-top hamlet of Blore at 750 feet. Up here in this neglected country stands the 400-year-old Blore Hall, where the Bassett family lived until they died out. In the unassuming church across the lane is the unusual tomb of

William Bassett who died as the seventeenth century dawned. The chapel in the north-east corner is virtually filled with what has been described as 'an enormous bed' with the recumbent Bassetts lying there between headboard and foot.

Up the slope to the west stands the conical 1,100-foot hillock topped with its conspicuous plantation called Hazelton Clump. It is to southern Peakland what Chanctonbury Ring is to the Sussex Downs. From this windy belvedere there are great prospects in clear weather up the Lower Manifold and into the mouth of Dovedale with its mighty portals of Bunster Hill and Thorpe Cloud. Behind that are the jumbled hilltops of this limestone land, range upon range of pale hills punctuated here and there by isolated plantations. Far away to the north-west is the dark backdrop of gritstone country where Hamps, Manifold and Dove are born – between is the country traversed by these three rivers towards the lowlands.

Sunbeams on the Cheshire Plain

If you want bleak and forlorn-looking landscape, go to the broad Staffordshire moorlands on a grey day. That countryside where the Dove and Manifold have their sources rises to over 1,800 feet on Axe Edge; it was the last wild country to be 'taken in' by agricultural improvements in the last 250 years. Much of the higher intake land here is on the very fringe of what can be viable; some of it has reverted to heather and rush. Many of the little farms of blackened, rain-washed gritstone have fallen into dereliction.

Epitomizing this wind-racked, western gritstone moorland is Flash, claimed to be the highest village in England. It stands above the 1,500-foot contour on lanes which lead steeply westwards into the gorgeous wooded corners of the Dane Valley. Come to Flash on a January day and you will get some idea of the invigorating life on these tops. There may be an east wind blowing and the smell of snow in the air; the Swaledale-cross ewes will be sheltering where they can behind a black and tumbled wall. There is little protection up here on the open heights, but in summer the churchyard trees give that corner of the village a surprisingly lowland look. Not so, though, in winter when the icy blast moans through the skeleton branches and rain wets the house-sides.

A mile or so to the south-west of Flash village lies dank and boggy Goldsitch Moss, centre of a remote outcrop of coal measures. The rim of the basin is the lofty upthrust of gritstone rock called the Roaches (literally, rocks) on the western side and dramatic Ramshaw Rocks to the south-east. Goldsitch Moss was a productive coalfield a long time ago; its fifteen or so workings supplied the local population and gave employment where these semi-sterile farms made for a hard living.

I see, in my mind's eye, horses and carts being loaded with coal. Stooping, Lowry-like figures throw shovelfuls of the black stuff;

The Torrs, New Mills

others fill sacks and stack them under a ramshackle shed. Mud lies all around and a curlew calls. This was the measure of the Goldsitch and district coal-mining industry, small, amateur and difficult – no wonder it failed so completely. If you look around today, you may find a spoilheap surrounded by oozing bog but little else.

Chapel steps, Flash

The Black Brook drains Goldsitch Moss, tumbling westwards to join the River Dane near Gradbach. The Dane is one of the loveliest little rivers in England and chatters on through its wooded gorge eventually to wind out across the Cheshire plain.

Goldsitch Moss

Wincle Grange

Wincle village, of pretty name and countenance, lies on the steep-angled valley-side above Danebridge. Few people discover Wincle Grange, one of the most fascinating buildings in all Peakland and certainly one of the oldest farmhouses in the southern Pennines. Combermere Abbey, a Cistercian house far away across Cheshire near the Shropshire border, was granted this land in the twelfth century, sufficient pasture for 2,000 sheep and their lambs. The monastic grange was built here on top of the ridge above 900 feet. The farmhouse we see now is the fifteenth-century one which replaced the original. Its architecture has ecclesiastical connotations – look at those lovely windows on the north-eastern side, and the pink sandstone of its rebuilding was quarried nearby. No roads spoil the old-world peace at Wincle Grange, and we can look out to the west, across the broad trough of the Shell Brook to the whaleback of Minns hill, which must be unique in having one name for its eastern side – Wincle Minn – and another for its western flank – Bosley Minn. This broad hill was part of the Wincle Grange estate and provided summer pasturage for the great Combermere flock eight centuries ago.

A footpath goes south-westwards from Wincle Grange towards the Shell Brook and passes the semi-ruinous Dumkins. This amazing half-timbered farmhouse was lived in until the mid-

1950s. Constructed in the fifteenth century using four tree trunks, it was the home of the pioneer settlers who cleared the woods of these lower valleys and began to farm them. No other dwelling of this sort remains intact, and because the preservation order on Dumkins precludes renovation, the pretty place slowly tumbles down. It is high time that common sense allowed proper renovation here.

Up on the southern end of Minns Hill stands Hawkslee Farm, formerly part of the Cistercian Wincle estate. Cattle and sheep still graze the broad pasture on the ridge of Minns Hill, and right along its top runs the tarred public lane which gives broad vistas in every direction. All along the western fringe of the Peak District, especially in Cheshire, the high ground falls suddenly to the plain so that the views are broad and dramatic. This Minns Hill-top is the southernmost Cheshire belvedere, looking three miles to the Cloud in the south-west, with Congleton to the right, beyond its rocky prow. The grazing animals on this grassy ridge usually make good foreground subjects for photographs.

The next hill to the north is sixty-four feet higher, called Croker Hill and now supporting the horrid 286-foot telecommunications tower. What a sight it is, what a monstrous intrusion on the landscape. Its true scale may be judged by noting the size of adjacent Lingards Farm!

Cheshire's Gritstone Trail (a long-distance footpath developed by Cheshire County Council) runs from Hugbridge, where the Leek–Macclesfield road (A523) crosses the River Dane, and comes over Minns Hill and Croker Hill and northwards by Teg's Nose Country Park to end at Lyme Park (about 18½ miles).

Croker Hill is the highest part of the great mass called Sutton Common, broad, rough pasture upon smooth hill slopes with great views over the Cheshire Plain and eastwards to the crumpled gritstone escarpment above Wildboarclough and Macclesfield Forest. Shutlingsloe's unmistakable cone, three miles distant on that eastern horizon, is one of Peakland's few peak-shaped hills.

On the gentle descent of Sutton Common from Croker Hill the green hollow ahead is the valley of the River Bollin as it winds through Langley and Sutton Lane Ends. Beyond is the rude sprawl of Macclesfield. All this lovely landscape of open common, brown moorland and deep valleys and tree-dotted plain is Tunnicliffe country.

When Charles Tunnicliffe was born in 1901, his parents were living in a small terrace cottage in the east Cheshire village of

Telecom Mast on Croker Hill

Langley, nestling close under the western slopes of the Peak District hills. In 1903 they moved to Sutton Lane Ends, a mile to the west, out at the edge of the plain. Here father Tunnicliffe – a cobbler by trade – became a small farmer, and here his family of four girls and a boy grew up. No one at that time, over eighty years ago, could imagine that the only Tunnicliffe boy would become one of the world's finest wildlife artists. In *My Country Book*, his first book, published in 1942, Charles Tunnicliffe explained that he had no idea what caused him to take paint and pencil – 'What is it which compels one man to be a farmer, another a wheel-wright, and another a driver of trains?' What is certain, though, is that the small world of Lane Ends Farm, at Sutton, the steep country behind it and the open spread of the Cheshire Plain to the west did influence his subsequent work when he began to draw and paint. He remembered chalking on the freshly creosoted wooden cartshed near the gate, and drawing all manner of farm animals on the whitewashed interior walls of the cowshed and stable.

From an early age Tunnicliffe had to work hard and long on the farm, so he knew what the subject of his artistry was all about. Until he was nineteen he worked at home and attended first the local school then Macclesfield and Manchester Schools of Art. A scholarship to London's Royal College of Art meant a complete change for the young countryman whose heart was ever in the east Cheshire hills. Much of his finest work – etchings, watercolours, woodcuts and oil paintings – is clearly set in this delightful corner of England, if we take the trouble to analyse the detail, the hill shapes and the sheets of water, the distant farm buildings and the curve of the narrow lane.

The farm was sold after the death of his father in the mid 1920s, but Tunnicliffe returned at last, in 1928, to live in Macclesfield, and he married Winifred Wonnacott, a fellow artist, a year later. In 1947 they moved to Malltraeth, on the west coast of Anglesey, his final home beside the sea and surrounded by the world of things he best liked to paint. The white-painted house of 'Shore-lands' looks out over a terrace where Charles Tunnicliffe once planted wild thyme between the stone slabs. Beyond the terrace is the broad sweep of the tidal estuary of the Afon Cefni. Here come a myriad waders and seabirds in winter, and the large frame of the artist was a familiar sight striding out on the embankment above the tidal flats and beside the straightened course of the river towards the railway viaduct. For the rest of his life Tunnicliffe worked in a veritable naturalist's wonderland, close to the sea and the call of the gulls, the spring song of the lark and the croaking of bogland frogs on summer evenings.

Even so, his heart was ever far away in the east. There in the chequered landscape of fields which still tilt on the western side of the southernmost Pennines, I remember his telling me, in 1974, that east Cheshire was his only true home.

'Why don't you go back?' I enquired.

'I couldn't,' he replied, 'because it means too much to me. Everywhere there is change and I've been told of some of the post-war changes at home. There's that housing estate in the Home Field, a Post Office tower on Sutton Common – they've ruined it all!' There were tears in his eyes. 'And worst of all, there's no one left who knows me. No, I couldn't ever go back. It would be too much – I'll keep the dream intact.'

How has this part of western Peakland fared in the years since Tunnicliffe left it? Would he recognize the old corners, the landmarks which he continued to use in the backgrounds of his work?

When I was traversing this country recently, the lowest reservoir at Langley lay radiant under a bright morning sun. A heron stood motionless near the far bank, and a family of moorhen paraded through the floating persicaria leaves which fringed the near shore. It was a scene which the young Charles must have seen countless times, quite unchanged even to this day. The upper reservoirs, though, are now surrounded by tall conifers, planted on the steep ground below Forest Chapel forty and more years ago. These gloomy woods now hide the remains of the old hill farms, such as Ferriser and Coombs, and their stone-walled pastures.

Not far below that little, lowest dam stand the quaint rows of cottages in Langley. Some are three-storeyed and were the homes of silk-spinners; now they are characterful village dwellings, and in one of them, beside the Dunston Inn, the Tunnicliffe boy was born. I am sure he would still recognize his first home but would be upset to see a gleaming estate of private houses directly across the road where a steep pasture stood only a very few years ago. It was here, on a windowsill of one of these three-storeyed cottages, that I first saw, twenty years ago, an inverted glass jar containing jam intended to catch wasps in the old way.

On now, under the trees and along the winding lane to Sutton, where St James's church stands atop its little mound. There has been little change here: the blunt broach spire is still conspicuous above the trees and cottage roofs, the same spire rising in the background of so many of Tunnicliffe's works through the years. It is there as a dark blue shape in the distance at dusk in his *Barn Owl at Twilight*, a great, bold composition with more than a touch of magic there under the trees at the edge of Sutton; it is there, the little point above the village, in early sketches in *My Country Book*, as a reminder of his several boyhood years in the choir, a homely beacon which he often added to his work as a sort of reassurance.

Judy's Lane winds down below the church and into Lane Ends where the Tunnicliffe farm still stands near the crossroads. As I walked down that way, it was easy to imagine the place un-changed for almost a century. Certainly there has been little sudden evolution here since the young artist played in the stream under the bridge or made for the hills with a sketchpad. The gable end of the barn at Lane Ends Farm is now re-pointed and possesses a memorial tablet to the artist's memory (unveiled by his younger sister, Dorothy Downes, in September 1981).

The Home Field in front of the farmhouse and yard was the scene of many early and middle-period works. As I write this, for instance, I look up at one of his engravings – *The New Calf* of 1928 – in which father and mother Tunnicliffe have just lifted a new calf into a sack-lined barrow. The proud parent is licking the calf before it is wheeled off across the thistle-dotted pasture to the farm, seen in the background with the spire of St James's beyond. Yet that field has gone forever, under a red brick estate of houses. Although the service road is called Tunnicliffe Avenue, one can easily understand the artist's sentiments when he said he cared to 'keep the dream intact', never to return to see the reality of a vanished world.

I went on with a heavy heart, out towards the plain, into the cool shadows under the lowland trees. Then, in no time it seemed, I was crossing the Macclesfield Canal on a swing bridge at Oakgrove. A girl was feeding a family of mallard from the towpath; little had changed here, though no horses now tow barges. On again, across the lush grasslands to Gawsworth of unchanging countenance, the unspoilt village of Old Hall, grand church and rectory and pool.

There is the avenue of elms and limes which Tunnicliffe loved, and along which he so often walked towards the village. 'There is an air about the place which attracts me,' he wrote in *My Country Book*, 'whatever the time of year.' He came here to look at and draw the waterfowl in particular, but he also drew and painted the buildings. In a drawing of the Old Hall and pool we see the wooden railings in the foreground, a pair of mallard drakes

Cottages at Langley, near Macclesfield

pursuing a single duck across the dappled surface beyond, and the attractive half-timbering of the great house behind that. That fencing remains to this day; the pool is still home for a rich variety of waterfowl, and the Old Hall is still visited by the ghost of Shakespeare's Dark Lady, Mary Fitton – and by hundreds of visitors in summertime. Luckily Tunnicliffe's plea of forty years ago, that 'the jerrybuilder never lay his vandal hands on this place', has not gone unnoticed. He would recognize Gawsworth still, and be happy with the lack of change there.

Turning back towards the hills as the day matured, I saw them rising as a blue curtain behind the tall trees of the plain. I climbed up the western slope of Sutton Common with the lowering sun on my back: Sutton Common, where the hill sheep, grazing amongst the gorse and rabbits, cast long shadows just as they had over sixty years before. An angry stoat was chasing rabbits back to their burrows exactly as one had on a summer evening when the young Tunnicliffe had come here to sketch. He recalled, too, the repeated efforts made to draw to his satisfaction the grand vista of the Cheshire Plain from the hill slopes above Langley and Sutton.

'Often have I been fortified by mugs of tea, which the kindly Ethel of Lee Farm has brought to me at my labours,' he remembered, and added that he believed 'the farm folks were a little sorry for me,' and often commented that 'Charley 'ud be better attendin' to th' farm; a dunna think ee'll mak' much o' this artist business.'

On summer Sunday evenings he would often saddle the black mare and ride up into the hills to gaze at that broad landscape of forty miles of plain, punctuated by countless hedgerows and woods. That landscape often appeared as the backdrop of etchings, woodcuts and watercolours. The 'dim blue ridges, one behind the other' of the Welsh mountains rose above the plain as we looked, too.

The only feature which the artist would not enjoy in all that view is the profile of Jodrell Bank radio telescope, ten miles out upon the flatlands. I finally stood atop the ridge and saw the steep Pennine slopes and age-old farms lit by the setting sun.

From this distance the countryside of one of the twentieth-century's greatest artists looks remarkably unchanged. He died on Anglesey, early in 1979, without coming back here, but had he done so, I'm sure he could have come up here, above Lee Farm, and still have kept the dream intact.

One of the friendliest hill roads in all of the Peak District is that which traverses the western hills between Whaley Bridge, in the

Goyt Valley, and Macclesfield. It goes up and down, in and out, connects such attractive villages as Kettleshulme and Rainow and gives broad views over the westernmost hills to the spread of the Cheshire Plain and beyond. This route – the B5089 – climbs out of Macclesfield, crosses the canal at Hurdsfield (an eastern suburb of the town) and twists on to Rainow. This latter is a long village, predominantly of lovely local stone; it is a model for the twentieth-century planner of how to use what can be quarried nearby and create varied and attractive dwellings. But the local authority did not take real note and allowed a shocking modern development in the pretty pastures below the village. Luckily it is not easily seen by the passing motorist but for the rambler it is a different matter. Due west of Rainow, immediately across the little valley, rises the long eastern side of Kerridge Hill. This is a narrow, north-south orientated ridge with a footpath along its crest at about a thousand feet above sea-level. Anyone treading the short sward here is in for some remarkable views – not least, the shock of that Rainow estate gleaming and rude in the green valley below! Avert your eyes to better things. The far-flung plain spreads to the west, and in clear conditions you'll see fifty miles to the distant blue outline of the Clwydian Hills. Much closer is the dark, wooded profile of Alderley Edge, affluent commuterdom since the rail connection with Manchester last century.

From White Nancy, the bold, white folly atop Kerridge Hill's northern end, you look straight down onto Bollington. Here's a former mill town which happily keeps much of its ordinary, no-nonsense feel in its steep streets and close-packed stone terraces and corner shops. Long may the likes of Bollington remain, though most of its mill chimneys no longer pour forth their dark smuts and sharp smells.

Just south of Bollington and clinging to the western foot of Kerridge Hill is Kerridge, the little village which gives its name to the ridge. Every old building here is a work of art, fashioned from the beautiful gritstone, slightly pink-tinged, which splits so finely into slabs that the building courses are shallower than with most Peak District gritstones. This, allied to the deep-eaved roofs typical of these east Cheshire hills, makes for altogether well-proportioned architecture which falls easily on the eye. All local planners and architects should come to Kerridge as part of their training, to take in the finer points of the old-time builders.

Kerridge owes some of its appeal, of course, to its hillside site, looking out over tree-dotted hedgerows to Alderley Edge beyond the first sweep of the plain. The village was the birthplace of the eminent sculptor Alfred Gatley in 1816. One of his greatest works, *Destruction of Pharaoh and His Host*, was done in carved marble – not Kerridge gritstone!

Back on the Macclesfield–Whaley Bridge road a mile beyond Rainow we come to an especially good viewpoint when the lighting is good – ideal towards sundown between autumn and spring. Here at 1,100 feet, where the road approaches the Highwayman Inn near Big Low, you can look west over Kerridge Hill and Alderley Edge to the Clwydian Hills and see, halfway across the Cheshire Plain, the subtle line of sandstone hills at Peckforton, and there upon its isolated rocky cone the ruins of Beeston Castle. It is an unmistakeable feature of the Cheshire landscape. Away to the north-west you may make out the cooling-towers of Fiddler's Ferry power station on the northern shore of the Mersey, between Warrington and Widnes, twenty-five miles distant.

Shrigley Hall

As the main road winds on towards Whaley Bridge, the green valley of the Harrop Brook comes into view, below to the west. In it are a dozen half-hidden farms, and beyond them a suggestion of Bollington and the plain. Down there, a little to the north of Bollington, stands Pott Shrigley, as attractive a village as any in this part of England. There is the old church of St Christopher with its well-proportioned tower surrounded by deciduous trees; Pott Hall is a happy mixture of styles in gritstone (now a retirement home), and out of sight of the village to the north, hidden by a spur of Bakestonedale Moor, stands Shrigley Hall, an almost unknown mansion, really a stately home, the seat of the Brabazon Lowthers until 1928. The Old Hall was replaced in 1822–5 by the present Regency house of eleven bays and a porch with Ionic columns. It was sold to the Order of the Salesians of St John Bosco in 1929 and served until recently as their college. A large chapel was built in 1936–8, Philip Tilden's only religious building, and the stone for it was quarried near the main drive. Pevsner has described the chapel interior as a 'piece of imaginative and resourceful spatial planning'. The Salesians left Shrigley Hall in 1986.

Less than three miles to the north-east stands Lyme Hall, a much better-known house in its broad park, and the home of the Leghs for exactly six centuries. Robert Legh, third Lord Newton, gave Lyme to the National Trust in 1946, and it is leased by Stockport Corporation. The house, gardens and park are open to the public. Come here and see the waterfowl in the formal gardens on a sunny winter's day or stride the breezy Cage Hill to the towering prospect tower of Lyme Cage, built about 1525. The National Park boundary has been drawn to include all of Lyme Park, protecting it from the suburban sprawl which edges this way from Poynton, High Lane and Disley.

As the B5089 gets nearer Whaley Bridge, it climbs ever higher, reaching 1,120 feet at Charles Head, where it suddenly twists down towards the valley of the Todd Brook. From Charles Head there is this quite sudden view, too. It spreads away to the north-east, beyond the unseen clutter of the Goyt Valley in the neighbourhood of Whaley Bridge to the far ramparts of highest Peakland. The western flanks of Kinder Scout fall from the 2,000-foot contour to the Sett and Black Brook valleys. Illuminated by a late sun after rain clouds have dispersed, this upland panorama can be both colourful and very dramatic.

A mile east of Charles Head is Kettleshulme. This old Scandinavian place-name perhaps derives from one Ketil who settled here at a 'hulm' – a watermeadow. Certainly a trickle of Danish settlers came to this western side of the southern Pennines about AD 900 and left evidence of their coming in a handful of names like Kettleshulme. Here, too, are the narrow-coursed stone walls of cottages and farmhouses, and the broad, well-proportioned roofs. The motorist will have no time to see them on his headlong dive across country. He will not see the date-stones or the mullioned windows, the cottage gardens or the ducks in some muddy yard. He certainly won't manage a conversation with some friendly cat or other. These are pleasures he must leave to the pedestrian.

So much for the journey between Macclesfield and Whaley Bridge, where the Todd Brook and Black Brook join the Goyt and the A6 thunders through (soon to be diverted along the Whaley Bridge and Chapel-en-le-Frith bypass). Early in the last century there was hustle and bustle of a different sort, for the Cromford and High Peak Railway had its northern terminus here. It was opened in 1831, to connect with the Peak Forest Canal which came up the Goyt Valley from Marple and Dukinfield. The high ground east of Whaley Bridge rises to the conical hill of Eccles Pike (1,213 feet), literally 'church pike' or hill. Obviously its sharp profile was attractive for prehistoric worship. In more recent times – 1937, in fact – six acres of its little summit were presented to the National Trust as a celebration of King George VI's coronation. So it is that we can forever stand on this open hill-top and look out in all directions, a busy view of semi-industrialized valleys and lots of many-faceted hills.

Just across the valley of the Black Brook to the north stands Chinley Churn (1,480 feet) tilting up to the east and presenting its gentle back to Goyt's Dale. No hill shape in the south Pennines shows to better advantage the effect of erosion on an anticline or upfold. The steep, stepped eastern face of Chinley Churn has been quarried; it produced good roofing slabs and paving stones, and it is still interesting to walk up through the gorse bushes above Cracken Edge and see the hard-won stone and quarry waste. From this path through the quarry you get as fine a picture of south-western Kinder Scout, of South Head and Mount Famine and back towards Chapel-en-le-Frith – 'Capital of the Peak' – to the south-east as you could hope for. I have looked out from the windy summit of Chinley Churn on a December afternoon and seen remarkable red sunset clouds rolling over Kinder Scout's 2,000-foot western rim. Then, looking away for ten seconds, I have looked again and the display is over, replaced by cold, grey cloud billows which sent me running down to Chinley station in time for the train. The atmospherics on this side of the main Pennine watershed are never static, and the colours on this western flank of highest Peakland change from hour to hour, sometimes from one minute to the next.

The little streams which come down off these west-facing slopes behind Chapel-en-le-Frith and Chinley join to form the Black Brook, its water originally used by several mills in the valley-bottom near Chinley. The higher country where the streams are born is a delightful contradiction of bleak slopes and wooded dales-country. Bagshaw is a little-known hamlet whose warm, brown cottages cling to a steep slope. It exudes great antiquity – which is not a surprise, after all, when we realize that this was one of several cores of early settlement in medieval times. Up to this time the area was likely to have been uninhabited but yeoman farmers settled here and imposed pioneering husbandry, a pattern still visible to the trained eye. A record of 1251 calls this hamlet Baggesawes (meaning probably 'badger copse'), and from it an illustrious family took their name. The lowest dwelling in Bagshaw is the Hall, once a much larger place and now a comfortable-looking farmhouse with its old-time yard and poultry still scratching amongst the brambles.

In the next deep valley to the north stand Ford Hall and its satellite hamlet. William Bagshawe bought Ford from his relatives the Cresswells in 1600, and his eldest son, also William, rose to fame as a leading Nonconformist. Much to his father's disgust William Bagshawe the younger became a curate in Sheffield. In 1652 he was appointed vicar of Glossop but was driven from his living along with two thousand other ministers by the Act of Uniformity of 1662. He sought and found seclusion at Ford Hall and succeeded to the property in 1669. Here he carried on his zealous work, walking long distances to preach in Peak District villages between Hucklow, Chelmorton and Charlesworth, his missionary ventures complemented by a series of theological treatises, described even eighty years ago as very boring.

Ford Hall, near Chapel-en-le-Frith

For forty years Bagshawe (who became known as 'the Apostle of the Peak') carried on his quiet ministry and never really fell foul of the law again. He opened a chapel at the tiny hamlet of Malcoff, half a mile beyond Ford Hall, but that has long since gone, though the collection of farms maintain their steep perch directly above the western mouth of Cowburn Tunnel, where Chapter 3 ended.

After William's death in 1702 came a line of worthy Evangelical Bagshawes, and to the original Elizabethan house was added in 1727 a grand five-bay Georgian portion. Then Samuel Bagshawe came into possession, a 'spendthrift dandy' and associate of George IV when Prince of Wales. His debts mounted and the estate was stripped of most of its assets. Then he reformed and retired to Ford, now almost a ruin, where he eventually died. The place was eventually restored, and one Reverend William Bagshawe added to the south front about 1845 using his own 'bastard Gothic' design. There have been bits added this century but the entire building (described by Pevsner as 'a Mixtum Compositum') is not a planning disaster: it somehow looks quite satisfactory, and in recent years much time and money have been spent on it by a new owner.

Ford Hall, its stables and adjacent dwellings sit well in their steep clough, enhanced by a surprising wealth of mature broad-leaved trees. From the high ground to the east, where a public footpath traverses at 1,300 feet towards Roych Clough and South Head, one gets a grand impression of this upland estate, its steep pastures and imaginatively placed shelter belts of sycamore and beech which slant down, breaking up the park-like grass fields – they must have cost a lot in time and cash to plant during the nineteenth century.

Mention of South Head, that shapely 1,600-foot-high cone to the north of the valley of the Black Brook, brings us to a view into the meandering clough of the River Sett. I remember an early summer morning when we went along under the broad, blue sky and a curlew and dunlins began their piping. The first cotton grass blooms dotted the moors where they tilt down to the west.

We paused on this delightful day upon the summit of South Head and gazed towards the north, where the brown-headed moors tumble from Kinder Scout and where the Pennine Way goes along the horizon by Ashop Head and Mill Hill. In the seven miles from its boggy source at Edale Cross to its confluence with the River Goyt at New Mills the Sett falls 1,350 feet.

Having tumbled more than 1,100 feet in the first four miles to Hayfield, the Sett adopts a leisurely pace along its broader lower

The River Goyt in the Torrs, New Mills

dale towards New Mills. Here today are the remnants of a once-thriving textile industry, mixed in with stone houses, dams and little hill farms. From the beginning of the eighteenth century the Sett Valley developed a spinning and weaving trade, based initially on the smallholdings of these hill farmers. It was the usual North Country story of thriving cottage industry looked back upon now as a particularly attractive economy before large-scale industrialization removed the last vestiges of Arcadia from most working folks' lives.

Here and there the three-storeyed cottages remain, the weaving rooms occupying the top floor. Nothing, though, stands still and the River Sett proved an ideal source of power as the eighteenth century progressed. Water-powered mills grew along the valley floor. After water-powered looms were developed in 1820, more mills were built and the cottage industry died away.

Alongside the spinning- and weaving-mills, calico-printing and paper-making were established. Then, in 1868, a railway branch line was opened between New Mills and Hayfield village. This three-mile-long single track carried passengers and freight for 102 years, and in the twenties it was common for as many as 5,000 ramblers to use Hayfield station on Sundays in summer. The familiar Class 13 and 14 tank engines hauled most trains, including loads of coal, cotton and timber for the mills and their finished products of fabrics, printed calico and paper. By the late sixties, trade had almost ceased and the Hayfield branch was closed to traffic in 1970.

That might have been the end of the story had not Derbyshire County Council seen fit to use the disused track as a traffic-free route for horse-riders, pedestrians and cyclists. In 1973 it was purchased from British Rail and work started to create the Sett Valley Trail. A car-park, picnic area and information centre were made on the site of Hayfield station, and as you go westwards towards New Mills the attractive juxtaposition of early industry, dwellings and hill farms is revealed through the trail-side trees. Moorhens are busy on the several millponds near the Sett, a heron often flaps lazily off from some secret reed-bed, and ducks make busy noises where the water flows beneath overhanging alders.

The Sett Valley Trail brings you into the north-eastern fringe of New Mills near Diglands and enters a totally unexpected gritstone gorge. The Sett swirls down here to join the Goyt at the heart of this deep chasm, called the Torrs. The place must have been even more interesting a century ago because it was the scene of considerable industrial activity. The earliest-known use of the name New Mills is in 1565, when a cornmill whose exact site has been forgotten was referred to as 'the Queen's Mill called Berde Mill or New Mill'. Late in the eighteenth century water-power was driving several cotton-spinning mills in the town, and the population was increasing as work became plentiful. By 1819 records show that there were eight spinning-mills, two printworks and two bleachworks, and thirty years or so later woven fabrics were being produced by power looms in several mills.

Old Mills in the Torrs, New Mills looking towards Lyme Park

The gorge of the Torrs was ideal for mill development: a rocky terrace immediately above river level, soft water for washing and dyeing, and weirs were easily built to give a head of water for power production. However, the Torrs had always been a hindrance to communication, and the first bridge had had to be built across the Sett immediately upstream of the gorge. The place naturally became the focus for the developing town, which spread up onto the high ground above the gorge but not into its shaded depths. Only with the development of mills in the gorge was a steep and narrow cobbled road made down to the river-side. Two narrow bridges were built across Sett and Goyt to make it easier to reach Newtown immediately across the Goyt.

During all this time raw materials for the mills, and finished goods produced in them, had to go up and down into the Torrs on the backs of packhorses and in small waggons hauled by other horses. Especially heavy loads were hauled up using an extra 'chain' horse kept in a stable near Torr Top Street. The Chain Horse House, as the stable was known, fell into ruins and was finally demolished in 1980 and is now a sitting-out area complete with commemorative plaque.

Old drawings showing the Torrs in its industrial heyday reveal an impressive grouping of mill buildings against towering gritstone cliffs. Torr Top Mill was a massive block of a building and is known to have been spinning cotton before 1794. About a century ago it ceased business but in 1904 linen-spinning was introduced, replaced by fustian-cutting in 1911. One year later a fire broke out and the spectacular blaze turned the Torrs into something reminiscent of a volcano's mouth. Difficult access hindered the fire brigade, and the mill was destroyed. Its foundations now perch beside the Goyt like some ancient castle ruin. The Rock Mill was next downstream, an assemblage of workshops ranged up the cliff-slope between river level and the town. This mill was a printworks for forty years, then in 1878 changed to paper-making. Four years later it was the scene of another great fire, and now we can wander amongst the few remaining foundations and wonder at the ingenuity of the mill-builders in such difficult terrain.

There was great activity in the Torrs when railways arrived after 1860. The line from Marple to New Mills was opened in 1865 and extended to Hayfield in 1868 – the route of today's Sett Valley Trail. A tunnel was driven through the gritstone cliffs to avoid the major curve of the Torrs. A second tunnel was built right under New Mills and carried Manchester–London trains from 1867. Today this is the main Manchester–Sheffield line through the

Hope Valley, and trains leave the tunnel immediately to cross the Sett on a viaduct.

The most impressive man-made feature of the Torrs area, though, is the lofty Union Road Bridge. It was a final solution to the problem of access between New Mills and Newtown on opposite sides of the gorge. This masonry viaduct was completed exactly one century ago and is one of the highest road bridges in this part of England. A pedestrian or motorist crossing Union Road Bridge might easily fail to notice the void below because of the high parapets but if you lean over on the up-stream side there is a dizzy view down to the site of Torr Top Mill and the remains of its 1846 chimney, hard against the backing cliff.

From the top of Station Road there is another dramatic view, down to the railway lines where they enter the tunnel with the surging waters of the Goyt far below. Rising above the far bank of the river is Torr Vale Mill, probably one of the original mills. It was spinning cotton as early as 1788, later producing a mixture of yarns, cotton bands and candlewicks and, since the beginning of this century, manufacturing towels. This mill remains as the last one actually producing textiles and has seen a change of power-source from the original water-driven wheel to steam in 1856 and electricity from 1931.

Here, at this viewpoint above the gorge, you can look out to the south-west, across hundreds of cottage roofs and factory chimneys, to the rearing blue profiles of the hills above Lyme Park in rural Cheshire.

Head of the Chew Valley

Cotton grass and Curlews

What is probably the deepest and most dramatic valley in the Peak District lies in Greater Manchester. The River Tame is a major tributary of the Mersey and flows southwards through its narrow and sinuous dale between Oldham and the lift of the high Pennines. The textile industry developed here, filling the valley floor and slopes with mills and terrace-houses, and perching churches at Mossley, Saddleworth and Delph. The largest tributary of the Tame, the Chew Brook, and its branch, the Greenfield Brook, come down out of their narrow valley, flowing westwards through cluttered Greenfield village to join the Tame near the sewage works below the Oldham–Holmfirth road (A635). One of the best ways to explore this dale is to take to the hilltops which virtually surround it, and walk round in a clockwise direction.

Immediately to the north of Greenfield rise the steep, stone-walled slopes of Dick Hill, its summit almost 1,500 feet above sea-level. Several steep lanes climb and cross up to Tunstead, where many of the dwellings still have long, many-mullioned windows to proclaim that they were formerly the homes of weavers. Throughout this damp upland district, a cottage textile industry flourished into the present century. One ivy-covered farmhouse above Tunstead has the names of the Shaw family and '1750' carved on a lintel.

Above these scattered dwellings a stony track continues to the top of the hill, known locally as 'Pots and Pans' because of the large hollows in the gritstone boulders near the summit. Though these basins are partly the result of natural erosion, tradition states they were scooped out by grouse-shooters to contain wine. The largest basin is 'Robin Hood's Bed', and local legend has it that the sick of the district were laid here in sacred water. In 1923 the Great War memorial was erected here to honour the men of the district. It must be one of the most conspicuous parish war memorials in the country.

Dick Hill is one of the finest viewpoints on this side of the Peak District, for there is an uninterrupted view to the south, into the ravine where the Chew Brook comes down from the high moors, and to the east where the Greenfield Brook curves round into the wilderness of Saddleworth Moor. Down below are the Victorian Yeoman Hey and Greenfield reservoirs, and the new and larger Dove Stone Reservoir where the Chew and Greenfield streams had their confluence. Beyond the deep, shadowed dale-bottom to the east is the extensive gritstone escarpment which is one of the most conspicuous features of the district.

By traversing slantwise down the slope towards the north-east, we gain the Oldham–Holmfirth road close by the mixed wood-land known locally as Bill's o' Jack's Plantation. This marks the site of the remote Moorcock Inn, called by everyone 'Bill's o' Jack's' because William Bradbury (son of John) was the landlord here. On a spring day in 1832 father and son were found dying after a vicious attack but, though several individuals were sus-pected, no one was ever convicted of this double murder. Ten thousand people attended the funeral at Saddleworth parish church. One hundred and three years later, 'Bill's o' Jack's' was demolished.

Going down through the plantation on a recent sunny day, when tits were chattering, we crossed the valley-bottom on the impounding wall of the uppermost reservoir and went steeply upwards for 550 feet to gain the edge of the plateau where the dark prow of Ashway Rocks emboldens the crest. Running for almost two miles to the south is a discontinuous edge of high gritstone crags which are among the highest and noblest in the south Pennines. Being on the western side of the main watershed, one might expect this dale to receive the greatest precipitation in the Peak District, but this is not so: the valleys of the Ashop and Alport some miles to the east record consistently higher annual figures than the fifty-one inches average here. In the past, though, these great gritstone edges did receive a massive amount of atmospheric pollution from Manchester and south Lancashire, so that climbers returned home looking like chimneysweeps and foundry workers. In recent years, of course, the widespread adoption of clean air zones has made climbing on these edges much more pleasant.

Striding on to the south we came, in half a mile, to a blackened cross on the crest of the plateau. It marks the site of the accidental shooting of James Platt, MP for Oldham, during a grouse shoot in August 1857. Keepers and beaters carried him down to his

Memorial to James Platt looking over Dovestone Edge

brother's mansion in the valley below, but he died two days later. The mansion is Ashway Gap House and was built as a shooting lodge for John Platt, textile-machinery manufacturer of Oldham, in the early 1850s. The cross and the house were designed by George Shaw, architect of St Chad's at Saddleworth.

The next gritstone edge to the south contains the mighty Dove Stone Rocks, formed of the 500-foot-thick series of coarse-grained sandstone known as Kinder Grit. Cross bedding and normal bedding provide the bulk of horizontal holds, and where the crags have been quarried, the holds and ledges offer sharper edges to the cragsman because they are less weathered by the elements. A few climbers visited Dove Stones before the First World War, but development of routes was only spasmodic until 1948. Only then was the true potential fully appreciated of what is now accepted as one of the most formidable and exposed climbing grounds in Britain.

Going on in the bright sunshine, we soon saw ahead, high on the top of the gritstone crags on Dove Stone Moss, the memorial cairn to two young local climbers who lost their lives while descending the second Sella Tower in the Dolomites in 1972. Far below, the brightly coloured sails of yachts were bending in the stiff breeze on Dove Stone reservoir.

In a further mile along the crest, we reached the place where the Chew Brook comes down out of its narrow ravine, overshadowed by some of the greatest upland slopes in the Peak District. Blocking the head of this ravine is the masonry impounding wall of Chew reservoir, at 1,600 feet one of the highest in the country. Work started here in 1907 and was completed by 1914. Chew Wells were said to possess medicinal properties but were inundated by the reservoir, together with the old house which stood close by.

Looking across the still waters of this lonely reservoir, we could see the brown plateau surface stretching far to the east, to Long Ridge Moss and Black Chew Head and the Blindstones. In midsummer these moors shine with countless cotton grass blooms, and the air is filled with the calls of curlew and dunlin. On that day, though, a skylark was singing overhead for all it was worth as we turned back towards the west, to follow the high ridge which hems in the south side of the Chew Brook.

The scenery here is dramatic, with huge slopes at steep angles, broken by several gritstone outcrops in an airy situation above the ravine's floor. Snow accumulates here in a severe winter, and on 20 January 1963 an avalanche of Alpine proportions occurred in Wilderness East Gully. Two expert climbers (one of them the author of the climbing guide for the Saddleworth–Chew area) were carried away and died beneath hundreds of tons of snow and ice.

In August 1949 there had been a greater tragedy nearby. A Belfast–Manchester airliner approached Ringway Airport too low and crashed into a gully on Wimberry Rocks, not far below the plateau-top. Twenty-four passengers and crew were killed, and remains of the Dakota can still be found at the crash site, below Wimberry Moss, where the high heather moors protrude north-westwards in the bold spur of Alphin Pike.

Now we turned down from the tumbled boulders and into the mixed woodland of Chew Piece Plantation and on by the edge of the new Dove Stone reservoir, where the sailing boats were being drawn out for the night. The water authority was faced with immense opposition from climbers, ramblers and many outdoor societies when this new reservoir was planned. Particularly vociferous was the Greenfield Paper Mill, which manufactures ninety-five per cent of all cigarette paper used in Britain. The site for the mill was originally chosen because of the adequate supply of good water, but the new reservoir threatened to inundate the factory's own waterworks. It was stated that this problem changed the project 'from an engineering dream into a legal nightmare'. Eventually all parties were satisfied, and the new reservoir adds light and life to this deep Peakland dale.

To the north and north-east of the Greenfield Valley is the wild, heather country of the northernmost Peak District. It is some of the loveliest and least-known territory of the region, offering space and great skies and miles of uninterrupted going for the real rambler.

The people most likely to tread this way are those following the beaten path of the Pennine Way, usually from south to north because most parties start at Edale and finish somewhere to the north – not always at Kirk Yetholm beyond the Scottish border, which was their original goal. After crossing Longdendale the official route originally went up Hey Edge to the east of Crowden Great Brook, a direct and safe way up to Black Hill in misty conditions. Since 1966 the recognized path keeps to the west side of the valley, following the popular path to Laddow Rocks, then swinging round for an indistinct and tedious trudge across ever boggier ground. Black Hill's summit is broad, black and usually hard to cross on account of its acres of oozing peat. A. Wainwright claims no other Pennine summit has such peat, naked and unashamed, and that no other shows such a desolate and hopeless quagmire to the sky. On dark days, when cloud-rolls hide the sun or mists destroy all views, this is a depressing high point of the Pennine Way (1,908 feet) but on frosty, blue-sky winter mornings it is an invigorating spot, and rock-hard ground promises easy going in any direction.

Up here, in 1841, was discovered the wooden framework of the thirty-six-inch Great Ramsden theodolite set up here in 1784 as part of the original triangulation of the country. Jesse Ramsden (1735–1800) went from his native Yorkshire to London in 1755 and three years later became apprenticed to a mathematical instrument-maker. In 1762 he set up in business making astronomical instruments and soon gained an enviable reputation for the high quality of his products. The theodolite used here on Black Hill two centuries ago now stands in the Science Museum, and a standard concrete triangulation pillar occupies the same highest point of what Wainwright calls 'this acid waste'.

A recent man-made apparatus asserts itself rather more than Ramsden's theodolite a mile to the east of the summit. It is the slender Holme Moss television mast which so often touches the grey cloud bases. The original mast was erected in 1951, then the most powerful televison transmitter in the world, adding eighteen million viewers to the BBC's audience. A new mast has recently replaced that first one, 740 feet high and designed to radiate mixed polarization signals for improved radio-reception through-out the north. It was inaugurated when Fred Dibnah, celebrated son of Bolton, climbed to the top.

The broad top of Black Hill prevents views down into the many valleys which run up towards it, and anyone standing on the summit will find it hard to believe they are less than a dozen miles from Salterhebble, Ramsden's birthplace in the congested lowland near Halifax.

From this plateau-top two modern footpaths radiate towards the north-west and north: the former is the ill-defined line of the Pennine Way which in two miles reaches the Greenfield–Holmfirth road (A635) near the site of the notorious Moors Murders' graves; the other is the more popular Pennine Way Alternative leading by way of Wessenden Head into the reservoir-dotted Wessenden Valley and Marsden.

The main Pennine Way continues towards the north-west beyond the A635 high road, over White Moss where cotton grass waves in summer. Here runs the Cotton Famine Road of sad memory, created by starving textile workers when there was no work in the mills, carving out this east-west route with picks and shovels and so keeping themselves alive. The present (later) road allowed it to go back to nature, and only the sunken ditch, filled in by peat and heather tussocks, marks its presence now. Broom-head Moss and Black Moss follow, bleak and forbidding in bad weather, then the roar of traffic heralds the Standedge Cutting, where the busy Oldham–Huddersfield road (A62) crosses the main Pennine watershed. And there the Pennine Way really leaves Peakland, crossing over the National Park boundary and heading northwards for Millstone Edge and Blackstone Edge, which are beyond the scope of this book.

Those taking the lovelier Pennine Way Alternative down the Wessenden Valley soon come to Wessenden Reservoir and the interesting – though uncharacteristic – Wessenden Lodge amongst a luxuriant spread of rhododendrons and in view of a delightful waterfall, all very much in contrast to the open plateaux to the south and west.

Then comes Marsden, typical stone mill village of these York-shire valleys, with plenty of no-nonsense terrace houses and chapels and busy corner shops; a pleasant place to live. This is the terminus (or start) for the classic Edale–Marsden walk, the turn-round point for those doing the Edale–Marsden Double. The useful youth hostel was opened in 1975, using a defunct co-operative shop. There is an interesting textile museum, relating the story of two centuries of cloth-manufacture in the district.

The northernmost hill of the Peak District is Deer Hill (1,400 feet) overlooking Marsden and the narrow Colne Valley. It has a rocky outcrop called Shooters Nab, last crag in Peakland, with a steep view down to the north, across Marsden to Slaithwaite Moor and Scammonden.

The steep hill road which connects Woodhead, in Longdendale, to Holmfirth (A6024) climbs to 1,718 feet close to the Holme Moss television station. The broad, brown moorlands that stretch to the east of this road are less frequented than most of these northernmost heights. In summer they are dotted white with cotton grass, and the call of curlew and dunlin are commonplace, waders up from the sea coast and estuary flats to breed under the wide sky.

Ramsden Clough runs down to the north, as rocky and hidden from the general gaze as any in the whole Peak District. It is beautiful in shape, craggy and dark shadowed in winter, when the low sun never reaches its narrow floor, where a stream gurgles down to help fill the little complex of reservoirs at Yateholme. The several odd-shaped coniferous plantations around these waters often form a background to television's *Last of the Summer Wine* shots.

South Yorkshire's major river is the Don. It rises on the eastern flank of Withens Edge, at almost 1,600 feet above sea-level, and flows due east for eight miles until, beyond Penistone, it turns south-eastwards down an ever-deeper valley to Sheffield. Don Well is one of several springs which rise on these broad moors to swell the water draining off the peat in the typical groughs (channels cut by erosion). One of the upper Don's main tributaries is Dearden Clough, a small valley carrying water from Upper Dead Edge to the newly enlarged reservoir at Dunford Bridge. An Ordnance Survey map of 1843 refers to Dearden Clough – there is Dearden Dike, too, draining the clough, Dearden Moss directly over the line of Woodhead Tunnel, Dearden Spring and Dearden Foot Plantation of wind-bent, stunted conifers above the reservoir's western shore. I have always presumed that Dearden was a family name and that it was connected with my own relations – my great-uncle Hardress Dearden introduced the Blue or Mountain hare to the northern

Peak District from Scotland at the turn of the century – but that may not be so. 'Dearden' derives from the Old English term *deor*, an animal, beast or deer, and *denu*, a valley. So here is a valley or clough frequented long ago by, maybe, deer.

Dunford Bridge is a tiny stone hamlet, almost hidden from the world at the bottom of the valley where the Don gathers several streams before that long run to the east and Penistone. The hamlet has seen busier times. When the first bore of the Wood-head Tunnel was being driven to take the Sheffield–Manchester railway, the completed section right up the Don Valley brought passengers here. They then transferred to a coach which carted them over the moors to Woodhead, where they boarded a second train for the rest of the journey to Manchester. This scheme operated between July and December 1845, and Dunford Bridge's inn, the Stanhope Arms, must have done brisk trade for five months. As soon as the tunnel was opened to traffic on 22 December 1845, the hamlet settled back into relative obscurity (though the population was increased by station and other staff).

Another burst of activity came with the construction of the third Woodhead Tunnel between 1949 and 1953. Well over a thousand people were housed here in a temporary village im-mediately over the new tunnel mouth. After the tunnel was completed, everything was sold off and Dunford Bridge slum-bered again, only to become busy again when the new reservoir was built across the valley immediately upstream of the railway station and council houses. This great impounding wall now dominates the place, as do the giant pylons carrying high-voltage cables to the place where they go underground through the old Woodhead Tunnels.

Half a mile north-east of Dunford Bridge, beside the Penistone road, stand the rows of blue brick railway cottages called Town-head. They look highly incongruous here, something out of the back streets of an industrial town, not Pennine cottages. Here lived some of the men responsible for the maintenance of the Woodhead line. The cottages became redundant years ago and have been inhabited since by urban folk seeking a rural life well above the thousand-foot contour.

Further along the road stands Carlecotes, and suddenly we are in a different world. Though it is at 1,100 feet, this hamlet is well endowed with deciduous trees, especially in the grounds of the Hall. There is a reference to this spot as early as 1277, its name derived from Old English words meaning 'peasants' cottages'. There are still cottages here but the ancient Hall is the focus of interest, so well placed in its lovely garden that one could easily forget the inhospitable surroundings. The little church was built in 1857, its interior made dark by the use of much timber.

The Hall made the headlines in September 1971 when Messrs Henry Spencer & Sons sold its contents on the premises. Most of the furniture had been there since Georgian and early Victorian times. The most interesting lot was the Ceremonial Panoply of

The old Flouch Inn, near Langsett

Garter King of Arms Sir Ralph Bigland, who was appointed in 1780. The tabard (a knight's garment worn over armour) was emblazoned with heraldic emblems which included the White Horse of Hanover. It was purchased at the sale for the Royal College of Arms for £615. There were many unusual items at Carlecotes, things which had lain there for generations, some hidden away under dust and cobwebs in back rooms. One of these was a very large dog-collar worn by a great hound in one of Sir Edwin Landseer's paintings.

Carlecotes Hall has changed hands but the atmosphere of antiquity remains; with its surround of old trees and outbuildings it is an oasis at the edge of the northern moors, a forgotten corner missed by most visitors and travellers on the high roads to Holmfirth or Penistone or Woodhead.

From Carlecotes there is a public footpath crossing the fields to the south-east. At Softley – an old farm recorded here in 1593 with a name meaning 'soft or agreeable clearing' – a lane goes on to Hazelhead with its long-gone station where ramblers could leave or catch a convenient train on the Woodhead line. Alternatively the line of the path continues to the Barnsley–Manchester trunk road near the celebrated Flouch Inn. This is bleak and troubled country on a wild night, and many a traveller has had good reason to be thankful for the lights of the original inn (built about 1825 at the crossroads) or, more recently, of its rather flamboyant and inappropriate replacement across the road.

Forgotten Hill Farms

Pre-war ramblers may not have had legal access to the highest gritstone plateaux but they did explore a high country still well populated with genuine country people, an indigenous population whose predecessors had often lived there from the Middle Ages. The Edge family of Onecote was mentioned in an earlier chapter as having farmed in one place for eight centuries; they were not unique.

Quite suddenly, certainly since the Great War but more particularly after World War II, rural depopulation has completely altered the age-old pattern. Whereas pioneer ramblers like G. H. B. Ward, Fred Heardman and Donald Berwick could rely on a warm welcome at many remote farms and cottages in the high country, few such places remain inhabited – if they do, most of them have lost their original families or have changed their function.

Edale Head House was the first derelict hill farm I can remember seeing, high on the slope above the infant Noe near Jacob's Ladder. Its tumbled walls and flaking plaster suggested great romance and I determined to go there and rebuild it, high up on that windy hillside. Today it is just a tumbled heap of stones, bypassed by the crowds who flock this way on summer week-ends. But I still wonder about Jacob Marshall who lived here two centuries ago and made the steps up the gradient above the packhorse bridge leading to Edale Cross on the watershed. This was not just a philanthropic exercise, because Jacob carried wool from the Vale of Edale to Stockport, and his 'Jacob's Ladder' made it much easier to get up the hill alongside his farm. I have read that Edale Head House was haunted, and it would not be a surprise if that was true, but its tumbled walls do not provide much shelter these days – even for spirits.

Half a mile below Edale Head stands Lee House, a very old mini-settlement with trees for shelter and sheep wandering in the narrow lane. A little lower the Crowden Brook comes tumbling down its tributary valley from the edge of Kinder Scout to join the Noe at Upper Booth (one of the hamlets or booths mentioned in an earlier chapter). There is the smell of antiquity here. Crowden-lea is the beautifully proportioned stone house dating from 1587 and for a long time the property of the Shirts, an old Edale family. In Miss Greta Shirt's time Crowdenlea was quite unchanged and so authentically Jacobean that part of the Sixties film *Charlie Bubbles* was shot here. There are Shirts still at Nether Booth, the late Mrs Shirt being a notable authority and breeder of White-faced Woodland sheep which once inhabited the gritstone country in considerable numbers. The large, pale, plain-faced sheep which are descendants of pure-bred stock can still be seen here and there on the high ground.

Dr Mary Andrews of Shatton quotes the interesting account book belonging to John Shirt of Crowdenlea in her *Long Ago in Peakland* (first published in 1948). It gives a fascinating glimpse of everyday events on a gritstone hill farm in 1754.

John Shirt spent a shilling at Tideswell Fair, half a crown for a cattle drench. He received £1.12.6 for sixty-five pounds of butter sold in Sheffield, and £4 for twelve ewes. In the New Year his son Mark 'gave over going to school' at Chapel-en-le-Frith, while his son Jacky started school. Dr Andrews presumes they were weekly boarders for it would have been impracticable for them to cross and re-cross the lonely Stake Pass to Chapel-en-le-Frith every day.

Twenty years later we read that the farm labourer James 'went home badly' – that was in June; two months later he went back to work but two days before Christmas 'James fell ill again'. Farmer Shirt settled up with his ailing labourer and paid him £3. Poor James would receive no social security benefits and we can only guess at his fate thereafter. Mary was a maid at Crowdenlea at the same time. She received £3 a year plus 'a scarlet cloak, blue dress and pinafore with a pair of boots'. There was a tiny rear staircase to her humble bedroom where she would retire after long, exhausting days, her candle flickering on winter nights, ice flowers encrusting the tiny panes, and a draught under the oak door.

In the Woodlands Valley separating Bleaklow and Kinder Scout are many romantic farms, some abandoned like Bellhagg Farm, others still thriving. Rowlee is one of the latter, a substantial farmhouse rebuilt in 1849 by the Duke of Devonshire for his long-serving agents the Greaves family. The last Greaves left

Rowlee Farm, Woodlands Valley

Rowlee just before the Great War but it is still a working farm owned by the National Trust. Much painstaking repair is taking place in this part of the High Peak, and the National Trust is to be congratulated on its sensitive treatment of barns, cowsheds and dwellings in the skilled hands of Peter Eyre and his team of craftsmen. Their work at Edale End recently received a conservation award.

The construction of large-scale waterworks has had a tremendous effect on life in the loneliest gritstone country. The development of reservoirs in Derwent Dale and consequent de-population are well known but there are other places which have been just as badly affected. One such is the upper valley of the Porter or Little Don upstream of Stocksbridge. There is Underbank Reservoir just west of that town, then Midhope Reservoir and Langsett Reservoir nearest Langsett village with its inn, café and youth hostel by the highroad to Flouch crossroads, Woodhead and Huddersfield.

Sheffield Corporation owned most of the land in this valley, purchased to construct the dams and control the drainage basin. Their ill-informed policy of turning out all occupiers of remote habitations on the grounds of reducing pollution caused virtually all the lovely farms of the Porter to fall into decay. Some of these remain as romantic ruins; others were completely swept away. Though the policy of the Yorkshire Water Authority may be more enlightened, the damage has been done, and it seems unlikely that hill farmers will again inhabit this quiet country.

Any rambler traversing the wild country between Derwent Dale and the Porter Valley and on to the Flouch Inn will probably follow the ancient Cut Gate bridleway. Beyond the broad water-shed above 1,700 feet (immediately north of Margery Hill, South Yorkshire's highest point) the track dips gently northwards and reveals magnificent vistas over a great tract of Yorkshire. Up here in early summer, when the curlews are crying and dunlins pipe from peaty hollows, when the optimistic cuckoo's call echoes in Mickleden Clough, the great prospect is of paradise revealed. There are the shady moors to the west, the green valleys ahead, and a far jumble of woods and fields and a hundred imagined villages in the lowlands. Beyond, at the edge of the world, are the slender spire of Emley Moor transmission mast (Britain's tallest concrete structure) and the cooling-towers of power stations far out on the plain, Ferrybridge and Drax, sending aloft gorgeous man-made cumulus clouds to beautify the empty sky. From this distance it is all very much an idyll, open spaces and quiet sheep and that huge canvas behind.

The track is easy to follow on towards the north, gently descending the Midhope Moors. If you look carefully in clear weather, you can pick out traffic moving on the Woodhead Pass (A628) which climbs westwards for miles towards the 1,500-foot summit at Fiddler's Green and on to Longdendale and Greater Manchester. At the important junction where the Barnsley–Manchester (A628) and the Sheffield–Huddersfield (A616) roads cross stands the famous Flouch Inn. The original public house was opened about 1825, called New Inn, and its first owner was George Heward. He had a slough or 'flouch' lip, so the place gradually took on this nickname. The old Flouch was the stone house standing right on the side of the Huddersfield road, often the refuge sought by old-time travellers overtaken by severe weather or vehicle breakdown. Just before the last war it was replaced by the large, new building across the road, a place quite out of character in its setting, being more suited to a suburban housing estate.

The flat-roofed café near the crossroads has a notice in the window telling coaches to 'keep moving'. Its farmer owner travels widely in search of bargain fare – Barnsley, Penistone, even Leeds. Being a native of the place, he's seen most of the farming families fade or move from this once close-knit community.

On the way down Cut Gate towards the Flouch, we skirt Hingcliff Hill. Here a wall comes straight up from Mickleden Clough-bottom, straight for half a mile. It was built by John Beaver of Thurlstone about 1835 and he was paid at the rate of 1s. 6d. per rood of seven yards. Its local name, Dead Horse Wall, probably originated from the saying ''e were workin' on t'dead horse' – low-priced piecework. Poor John Beaver would be annoyed to see the condition of his wall nowadays: as with so many upland drystone walls, its upkeep is economically impossible.

The track soon curves down to the wooded bottom of the valley to cross the Porter immediately upstream of Langsett Reservoir on the rebuilt Brook House Bridge. Up the slope amongst the old deciduous trees stood delightful Brook House Farm, farmed about 1830 by Edward Appleyard. He once asked two lads to help him with the sheepwashing near the bridge, promising to give them a duck. This he did by pushing them into the river! An earlier occupant of the farm had to pay a rent of one snowball in summer and a red rose at Christmas. That was in 1588; by 1722 Isaac Wordsworth was only required to pay the rose at Christmas. The last occupant was Farmer Goldthorpe and he left about 1907, since when Brook House Farm first fell into disrepair and later was completely demolished so that all we see now is a level, grassy spot under those old trees above the river. If you look carefully on the rock outcrop beside the track down to the bridge, you will find some old initials carved long ago by the locals – maybe the Brook House children playing in the evening sunlight or lads from neighbouring farms out exploring after the day's work was over.

How Rocher is the earthy cliff overlooking the south side of Brook House Bridge, and Swinden Rocher is the steep slope 200 yards west of the site of Brook House Farm. The attractive wooded hollow where the Porter comes winding down from the moors is 'Swine Dean', a place where pigs were driven to forage for the plentiful acorns in autumn. This name evolved to Swinden and is used to denote this corner of the high country between Flouch and Porter. There were once six farmsteads – the first was Brook House, the second Swinden (sometimes called Near Swinden), 400 yards west of Brook House Farm. When G. H. B. Ward described these old places in the *Clarion Handbook* for 1938–9, he considered the south front of Swinden Farm 'one of the finest local moorside yeoman's dwellings'. The stone carved 'I.H. 1641'

The remains of Swinden Farm above the Porter Valley, near Langsett

referred to John Haigh who was buried at Bradfield in 1645. The east front dated from 1570. A photograph of this grand old farmhouse accompanying the article shows as nice a Jacobean building as you could wish for but in due course it was demolished and its stones still lie piled where they fell. Adjacent are a couple of most attractive outbuildings, beautifully proportioned and too precious to allow to collapse.

There were, in fact, two farms at Swinden, and the later house and its buildings still stand, though fast falling into ruins next to the site of the finer, disappeared farm.

A few hundred yards to the north, at the edge of the coniferous plantation which is engulfing the old pastures and scattered deciduous trees, are the remains of Far Swinden Farm. The date 1808 on a stone suggests a rebuilding on an ancient site because there were seventeenth-century mullions at the back of the house. The last farmer was J. Warhurst, who came in 1918 and departed in 1934, since when Far Swinden lay empty and more recently partially demolished, an act of legalized vandalism by an authority who should have known better.

The next farm was Swinden Walls, 300 yards west of the Flouch Inn and quite near the Woodhead road. It was, in fact, the precursor of the Flouch because it was a halfway roadside inn between Penistone and Woodhead. In the mid-seventeenth century John Shaw was the publican-farmer serving the drovers and carriers of leather, cheese and salt between Cheshire and Yorkshire. He was also useful in the crafts of 'horse-shoeing, saddling and elementary veterinary practice'. An old lady living at Swinden Farm in the late 1930s remembered Swinden Walls being farmed about 1870 when 'the rats came in and worried the pigs' ears'. It became unoccupied, like so many of the houses here, soon after Langsett Reservoir was completed in 1904.

The last place was Whiteley Farm, midway between Flouch and Brook House Bridge. It was last farmed by George Mitchell, who left about 1908. Its fields are now inundated by conifers of the waterworks plantation but its old drystone field walls still lurk amongst the trees. The farm has totally vanished.

As you come down Cut Gate from Derwent to the Porter Valley, a fine farm stands conspicuously among green pastures across the river. It is Hordron Farm, and for years I took it to be a thriving hill holding. Further up the valley stands tiny Upper Hordron at the end of its rough track below Long Moor Edge. In pre-war days G. H. B. Ward called them 'the last two outposts of the shepherd-farmer of the Little Don Valley'. They are early

English land settlements. Hordron (pronounced Harden locally) was the last of this pair to be inhabited; the house was vacated soon after 1910, and the farms were described by Ward as 'Cinderella lands, a testimony to the long reign of King Grouse and the later reservoir makers. It is sad evidence that many thousands of moorside acres today produce far less meat than before (and after) the legalized injustices of the Enclosure Acts, 1790–1830.'

Upper Hordron is totally abandoned but its high wall still shelters the grassy court from violent west winds. Hordron farmhouse stands semi-derelict but its yard and buildings and surrounding fields are still used by a neighbouring sheepfarmer. In fact, a new outbuilding has gone up; though the rural population has drastically declined, the size of holdings has increased and purpose-built structures are cheaper to erect than the old ones are to repair.

Upstream of Hordron stands a wooden shooting-cabin close beside the Porter, and just above that Loftshaw Clough meets Laund Clough – 'laund' is 'a channel or gutter for conveying water' (as in 'launder'). Overlooking Loftshaw is knobby little Wicken Hill, an eminence which bears few signs of the rowan trees which gave it its name. Laund Clough is unusual for the slanting exposure of gritstone slabs across which the stream runs down to the Porter. Ward put it well when he said, 'This long mile of lonely, shallow clough is a typical example of the moorlander naming a place according to its principal feature.'

Three hundred yards above its confluence with Loftshaw Clough stands Scarratt's Stone, close by the stream. On it is carved 'Scarratt's Stone, 1894'. Now Scarratt was a partner in a cutlery firm who lived in London, having spent his early life in Australia, and was a member of shooting parties here between 1887 and 1897. Such parties usually took lunch at the little cabin below the confluence, then walked up Laund Clough to the butts. This took about forty minutes but Scarratt, who was elderly, had a ten-minute rest at this stone, during which time he had a swig from a large whisky flask, so George Howson (of the Sheffield cutlery firm Harrison & Howson), who owned the shooting rights of these western Langsett Moors, had the stone inscribed in honour of his old friend.

Less than two miles east of Langsett village lies Midhope-stones, near the head of Underbank Reservoir. Prehistoric pottery has been found here, and by coincidence a pottery was opened here in the early eighteenth century. Since that time there has been a tradition of slip-decorated ware in this valley of the Porter. The name Hope here means 'enclosed land surrounded by hills', so Godfrey Bosville's verse accurately suggests 'a garden in a wilderness'. The name Midhopestones refers to the stepping-stones across the river near Dike-side Farm, now submerged at the head of Underbank Reservoir.

Upper Midhope is the hamlet at 900 feet west of Midhope-stones, a genuinely antique place at the edge of the wilderness which is certainly pre-Norman and naturally fortified. Quite unchanged, its fine stone buildings repay close examination, both for individual qualities and for the relationships of one to its neighbour. There are cruck buildings here, remnants of a building technique long since gone out of fashion but perhaps not quite so old as certain historians once believed. In her study of this building form in north Derbyshire and south Yorkshire (1970), the late Bessie Bunker considered the cruck building to date from maybe the seventh century, erected by colonizing Angles because they were familiar with traditional uses of timber construction. She believed that by the time of the Norman Conquest suitable oak timbers were difficult to find and this type of building went out of fashion. Other authorities think of the cruck building as a

Cruck barn interior

Hallfield overlooks the head of Bradfield Dale

medieval form, a theory now generally accepted. Here at Upper Midhope the barn at Well Bank Farm once had six sets of mighty crucks but now only five remain *in situ* because the other set were long since removed for use in a newer barn standing at right angles.

This part of England has maybe the finest collection of cruck barns. They extend in a broad belt along the eastern flank of the south Pennines. Mrs Bunker describes eighty-eight such buildings, a few of which have since been demolished, and there are one or two more which she did not discover. One such is the grand building adjoining Hallfield above Bradfield Dale, mentioned in an earlier chapter.

A feature of these fine buildings is the great harr-hung threshing doors, hinged on poles set in the floor and roof, on one of the long sides, which allowed a loaded harvest wagon to be pulled right into the barn. Opposite this is a smaller winnowing door through which the draught animals (originally oxen, later horses) could go when they had been unhitched from the wagon so that they could be hitched to an empty wagon and return to the harvest field for another load while men emptied the one inside the barn. The main purpose of the winnowing door was, of course, to cause a through draught when the corn was being threshed on winter days so that the chaff was carried away. All this changed with the advent of the mobile threshing machine and steam traction in the nineteenth century.

No one has described the old farming days in this corner of England better than Ivy Helliwell of Holmesfield. Her memories of a hard practical life are both poignant and amusing – the shame is that many younger readers just cannot fully appreciate the finer points of the way of life she recounts. The twentieth-century urbanite is increasingly ignorant of real country life; many of them seem nowadays to think of rural areas as a giant park laid out specially for their enjoyment. The hardships of earlier times are a closed book to the great crowd of townies, as are the simple delights and simple wisdom once enjoyed by their country cousins.

Miss Helliwell recalls her upright Aunt Kezsia who seemed to spend most of her life in prayer. When blackberry time came round, everyone was fed on blackberries – for breakfast, dinner and tea, then for supper, too. 'She would run to the hillside and quickly scoop up red, green and black ones into a basin' and return to give the children more of the plentiful harvest 'in a saucer with a bit of sugar on them'. At the week-end Aunt Kezsia would load the horse and trap with baskets of blackberries and bounce off to Sheffield to sell them to her friends.

Another surfeit of cheap food comes to mind when I recall the dread with which a certain farm labourer viewed the approach of the rhubarb season. As the crowns burst forth from the orchard sward, he knew that every pudding henceforward would contain rhubarb in one form or another. He was so heartily sick of the stuff that he would creep back to the farm under cover of early summer dusks to remove the upturned buckets from the sprouting crowns in an attempt to delay the start of the long season of rhubarb dumplings, crumble and, worst of all, bowls of the stewed stuff.

Life was hard and much of it was monotonous on the hill farms of long ago. For the hardy, seasoned rambler, though, the hill farms were picturesque places, busy centres of an age-old life style. At so many of them there was a warm welcome and simple hospitality. Many hill walkers became good friends of farming families in remote places.

A glance at the annual handbook of the Sheffield Clarion Ramblers highlights the welcome awaiting wanderers in those days: in 1935 Mrs Staton was offering teas, refreshments and hot water at Abbey Grange Cottage at the foot of Abbey Clough in Derwent Dale. At Barlow Woodseats Hall in the beautiful Cordwell Valley Mrs F. Botham was catering for 'Large and small Parties – up to 100. Speciality: Ham and Egg Teas.' Half a mile away across the fields at Mill Farm, Millthorpe, Mrs Towse was providing pots of tea for 6d. or hot water for those who brought their own tea-leaves, milk and sugar. Even after the last war Mrs Morgan, of the well-known threshing family at Barlow, was providing teas, pots of tea and ideal country apartments at The Cottage, Wilkin Hill, as she had for most of the twentieth century. Mrs Sweet was making pots of tea for ramblers at her remote cottage at Alport, off the Snake road, into the sixties. By this time, though, there were few offering these no-nonsense services, and today the rambler will be hard pressed to find a hill farm or cottage willing to mash a pot of tea.

Here and there we still come across a farm of the uplands which has seen little change, usually a scruffy holding with great evidence of neglect and abandoned possessions. Occasionally they come to notice when the farmer dies or retires and there is a sale of live and dead stock. The interest generated by such sales is usually in direct proportion to the length of time the family have resided there. Not long ago, for instance, an old-time farmer of the windswept limestone plateau near Monyash passed away and a variety of accumulated possessions was disposed of: machinery now of a collectable sort, beef cattle that should have gone to market long ago and a selection of semi-wild horses which the auctioneer's men are reputed to have spent a week rounding up in the surrounding countryside.

The town-dweller might wonder why some of these unchanging life-styles survive into the late twentieth century, why the long hours, scruffy stackyards and piled-up scrap machinery. Maybe it is the unworried, casual approach that is the wise way, better than the scrubbed yard and frenetic, gleaming white-painted wood-work which urbanites bring to the hills whenever they have a chance.

A Peakland Year

What we may see on explorations of this district is part of the complex tapestry of the rural year. To understand it in detail may take a lifetime; here are some things which come to mind as I think about a year here in the southern Pennines.

Sheep Sales, Besoms and Moss-Gatherers
The countryman's year really begins in autumn, beyond the harvest field. The natural year is ending, a new promise made with the sowing of winter wheat and barley.

There's nothing lovelier than the shine of the sun on newly turned furrows, where slices of clay alternate with sand and loam and small stones. Some folk dread the thought of coming cold, of wind or rain or driving snow, but the declining year – late September to December – is as grand a time as any, especially for the rambler on the heights.

John Clare knew well enough the loveliness of autumn; he loved to see the shaking twig dancing till the shut of eve, and the feather from the raven's breast falling on the stubble lea. His 'grunting pigs' were there waiting for the falling acorns, and the pigeons nestled round the cote. Altogether a cosy sort of time of year, no more so than when we come down to some sheltered valley from a day on the windy moors and see the first lights of evening and the smoke curling from a cottage chimney.

Keats asked 'Where are the songs of spring? Ay, where are they?' in his well-known autumn poem but immediately consoled himself with the instruction 'Think not of them, thou hast thy music too . . .'. Of course, the sinking year is just as grand as other times but we humans tend to look ahead and consider what this failing beauty must inevitably mean. Keats, though, looks on the bright side – at the touch of setting sun on stubble fields, at the robin's song from garden-croft, at gathering swallows and at full-grown lambs bleating loudly from the uplands.

Sunset from behind Stanage Edge

The hill country which we call the Peak District, in common with most others in Britain, is sheep country, and with the onset of autumn this means one thing. Sheep sales are an annual feature of the agricultural year – no more traditional country event can be found than these. By late September the lambs are big enough to be sold to lowland farmers; some are fat enough for the butcher, and the draft ewes are brought for a few years' further breeding on more hospitable lowland pastures.

Major sheep sales take place annually at Glossop, Hartington and Wildboarclough. The latter usually occurs on the last Saturday in September in the large, sloping field below Lord Derby's Crag Hall. Tall trees stand on two sides, and the shapely summit of Shutlingsloe looks down on the complicated system of pens formed by wooden hurdles where the worried sheep are confined. A motley crowd of farmers circulates, bending now and then to feel the amount of flesh under the fleece of a pen of promising animals. The auctioneers' numerous staff – men and boys – drive the newly arrived and loudly bleating batches of sheep through the maze to empty pens. It all looks most complicated but everything is usually ready for Ian Lawton (probably the region's best-known auctioneer) to start the sale dead on the stroke of eleven o'clock.

If you look carefully around at these upland sheep sales, you'll see many delightful facets of rural life that the townsman might think obsolete these fifty years. There's the red-faced farmer's wife enjoying a cup of tea at the refreshment stand, maybe one of the few days in the year when she gets away from the toil of the hill farm. A tall, lean sheepfarmer clad in greasy corduroy trousers held up with belt and braces prods a likely bunch of old ewes and passes judgement to his neighbour. Half a dozen excited farm children play around the pens; two lads throw sticks into the horse chestnut to fetch the conkers down – until a stick goes wide and hits someone near the refreshment stand!

On one recent Wildboarclough sheep-sale day the heavens opened and turned the sloping field into a quagmire in no time. All was gloom as cattle waggons became stuck in the churned-up ooze; the crowd melted away, only the serious bidders remaining in the damp shelter of the marquee where the soaked handlers attempted to keep the lots moving, urged on by Ian Lawton. The following year, though, brought soft September sunshine on the day and the mood was quite different. Golden Shutlingsloe looked down on the burnished tree tops as the last mist of morning drifted away. An hour later we were lying on that magnificent summit and gazing westwards over the Cheshire plain, making out the glint of the Mersey and the unmistakable profile of the Peckforton Hills and Beeston Tor almost forty miles away. Behind us rose Ian Lawton's amplified voice, clear as a bell 700 feet below, as the lots continued through the sale ring. By the time we came down through the trees to Wildboarclough at evening, the sale field was almost empty, just a few men loading the last of the sheep and dogs with lolling tongues lying in the dead leaves.

The biggest sheep sales take place at Biggin-by-Hartington. Each autumn there are several sales here between late September and early December. Biggin is an exposed little village, occupying flat limestone territory at almost one thousand feet between the Ashbourne–Buxton highway (A515) and the middle reaches of Dovedale. Pale stone walls criss-cross the countryside, with here and there a gathering of windbent trees. In poor weather it is a cheerless place, a scattered village where the winds blow unhindered from any point of the compass.

The second of the annual Biggin sales is held in early October and has the largest number of entries. In 1985, for instance, 20,684 animals were entered in Bagshaw's catalogue. The 217 rams are sold in a small ring to one side of the huge gathering of other sheep. Two auctioneers sell this multitude in two marquees while Mr Binder (of soft felt hat and plusfours) puts the rams through his little ring, entertaining the assembled company in the process.

'Come, come,' he admonishes his assistants who do battle with a recalcitrant Suffolk ram. 'We'll be here all night – get him in the ring.'

'I'm not selling the ewe lamb, only the Oxford!' he grins as a little girl leads her well-grown pet ram round the ring.

When the bidding is slow, he urges on the pace! 'I am selling the ram, gentlemen, not just the halter!'

A sheepfarmer returning to these sales from fifty years ago would certainly be surprised at the variety of breeds kept in the district now. In pre-war days he would expect to see the Lonk and Derbyshire Gritstone, a few White-faced Woodlands, some of the new Dales-Bred (fixed as a breed after 1930) and Swaledales. Now, though, there are Suffolks, Colbreds, Texels and tall, camel-like Blue Faced Leicesters, plenty of Swaledales and still a few Derbyshire Gritstones passing through the ram ring. As in most uplands the unique breeds of the district have been superseded by breeds from far away which give vigorous crossbred lambs when mated with indigenous ewes; the Suffolk may be a lowland breed but crossed with a hardy Swaledale or Gritstone ewe produces quick-growing lambs in the hills.

Here in the busy Biggin field where hundreds of countryfolk and thousands of noisy sheep mingle in seeming chaos we are not far from the place where a small dry valley cuts down to the south, into the solid limestone of the plateau, to form Biggin Dale. A path follows the bottom of this dale to come out on the banks of the Dove where that river flows out of Wolfscote Dale. The name of this latter, incidentally, has nothing to do with wolves – it was Wulfstan's cottage or cot. Likewise the origin of Biggin was 'niwe bigging' (which by 1244 had become Neubigging), literally 'new building' in Old and Middle English. What a contrast down here by the silent river with the noise of the sale up on the plateau; a few minutes for reflection below Drabber Tor, then we turn and return to the marquees, the barking auctioneer and the calling sheep, now being driven into the assembled transporters of their new owners. Some for pastures new, some for the butcher's slab.

Talk of moving sheep around the country reminds me that the theme of many shepherds' tales has been the strongly developed homing instinct of upland sheep. Regardless of breed this class of sheep is an extremely good route-finder, as typified in the following true story about a number of Penistone sheep.

In the early years of the nineteenth century a flock of Penistones were taken to Kent. Three of these animals soon disappeared from the fields of their new owner and could not be found. Eventually, though, two of the wanderers found their way back to their original home, a distance of 200 miles. When these animals died, their horns were hung in Hope parish church as a memorial to their tenacity and route-finding ability.

Farm sales, like annual sheep sales, are common about the time of Michaelmas (29 September) as many farm tenancies begin and end then. They can often be sad events, especially when the farmer is selling up because he is past work. I well remember, at a farm sale held on the eastern fringe of the Peak District years ago, an old man bent almost double with arthritis; it was amazing that he had managed so well for so long.

Bidding was brisk for the old cow and the Hereford heifers and a calf, and a good price was paid for each. Not so satisfactory was the interest shown in the odd tools and implements so useful on the small farm but no longer important to the modern farmer. The auctioneer was hard pressed to find a bidder for the butter churn, cream-separator, scythe and stone troughs. He failed to sell a red-painted bonny rake, that large handrake of long-ago haymaking. The bonny rake (sometimes eight feet wide) was dragged by hand over the ground to gather hay left after harvest in fields too small or too steep for a horse rake. Nowadays such bygones are sought by collectors, but not in those days.

An amusing note was struck when a pair of five-month-old Aylesbury drakes were put up for auction. The auctioneer pointed out that the ducks were, in fact, drakes and the bidding started. The old farmer, deaf as a post and concerned for his buyers' welfare, shouted out to the assembled company. 'Make sure on it – these birds aren't in lay yu' know!'

We were just about the last to leave the little farm, and as we looked back the bonny rake handle was showing above the stone wall that separated the stackyard from the misty hills. The old farmer hobbled back across his empty yard from his empty cowshed to the house with its smoking chimney. All life seemed to have gone from the place; like a school without children, a farm after a sale, when all the animals have departed, is a miserable spot – the spirit has gone out of it.

Not long after this I received a letter from an elderly lady who lived in a cottage in the remote hamlet of Moorhall, high on the edge of Eastmoor. She had a stuffed owl and wondered if I would like it as she was getting rid of unwanted furnishings since the recent death of her husband. On a dark, wild night I knocked at the old lady's door and was admitted to the cosy warmth of her parlour. From a dim corner she produced a well-preserved barn owl which stood in vicious attitude and appeared halfway through a meal of chaffinch (a leg of the unfortunate little bird was held aloft in the owl's cruel beak), the whole scene of attack covered by the graceful lines of a glass dome. I was pleased to acquire this piece of Victoriana, though it seemed a pity to be removing it from its rural surroundings where it had adorned the parlour so long.

As the lamp over the table hissed comfortably, the old lady asked me if I knew of anyone who might like her pianola. 'Now that Dad's gone, it seems silly to keep it – when someone might get pleasure from it,' she explained. The age of the pianola, that automatic piano of merry Sunday evenings of quieter years, has gone and I doubted at the time if anyone would want the instrument, just as few people would have wanted the stuffed barn owl I carried home later that night, beneath an October moon that now peered through the dispersing stormclouds. Since that time, though, pianolas and stuffed birds have come again into their own. The old lady would have no difficulty these days in finding buyers for these and other bygones which she was forced at the time to burn in her little garden.

Another October memory is of horseback days when we rode up on to the moor on a cold, grey afternoon on the gelding Harkaway and the lively mare called Shiela. Along the old lane, high above the Derwent Valley, all was quiet and as we passed Offerton Hall we could have been in another century – almost, anyway, for the sudden, shrill whistle of a locomotive on the railway far below could be heard above the clip-clop of Harkaway and Shiela on the stony lane. A plume of steam issued from the front of the train on the line between Hathersage and Bamford, for this was in the last days of steam-hauled traction. Now we left the lane and took to the muddy track through russet heather. There was a hovering bird over the moor ahead. We drew closer and were eventually in a position to look down the slope almost on top of the kestrel, the windhover of old, quartering this edge of the autumn moor for mice and voles.

The horses began to sweat as we climbed the steep slope and came onto the brow of Offerton Moor at over a thousand feet above sea-level. Up here it was even greyer than lower down, and the grey sheep paid little attention as we passed – obviously they felt quite safe as long as we remained in our saddles. It would not have been a surprise to see a witch go speeding across the tops of the heather in these drab conditions, astride a besom and cackling as she went. That the making of besoms was until quite recently a flourishing craft of eastern Peakland may come as a surprise in this age of foam-rubber mops and plastic-bristled brushes.

The best material for the 'bristles' is heather for 'soft' sweeping and silver birch twigs for 'hard' sweeping. Ash and hazel were considered the best wood for the handle, and split hazel for binding the 'bristles'. The only tools the besom-maker used were a besom grip (a round-jawed vice), to hold the twigs while binding, and a bond poker – a curved, spiked tool for pushing the free end of the bond underneath to tie a knot.

In the autumn each year the local besom-makers' yards were stacked high with heather collected from the moors. Besides making brooms for gardens, the besom men did a brisk trade until recent years in selling their products to the steelworks in Sheffield and Rotherham. Besoms were used there for sweeping up hot metal waste around blast furnaces because being relatively cheap they were expendable, and replacements kept the local craftsmen busy.

We later came down out of the curling mist, the horses pulling

Windgather Rocks near Kettleshulme

eagerly at the thought of Callow Farm and home. Lawrence Dungworth, ex-cavalry officer and one of the district's best-known horsemen, was still living there, and many people have fond memories of happy days spent in the saddle in this steep country west of the Derwent Valley; happy memories, too, of Lawrence and Alice and their family and sunshine in the slanting Callow farmyard with its incomparable view to Hathersage and Stanage Edge.

Mention of the farmyard at Callow reminds me of the muck-heap in one corner, unusual in that until recent years it contained such a high proportion of horse manure. It was a common thing in Octobers of long ago for the hill farmer to go out into the fields and woods to collect cart-loads of leaves, shed from his trees, and bring them to the pit in the yard. An old directory lists the sort of waste usually thrown into the farmyard pit in autumn: 'fern, coarse grasses, rush and flags, sweepings of kitchens, bones, ashes, woollen rags and yard scrapings'. Later in the winter this miscellany was covered by the manure and straw cleaned from the cowshed.

Even 200 years ago the value of a roof over the dung heap was appreciated, to prevent too many nutrients being washed away. The old directory advises: 'A slight shed should be thrown over the dungstead; and gutters should be contrived that all waste water and urine of the yard, oil dregs, greasy water and bloody water in which meat or fish has been washed should flow through them to the reservoir.' Not many manure heaps sport a roof these days because they get in the way when emptying them; instead a good proportion of the nutrients is still washed away by winter rain to pollute ditch and stream.

Autumn, and particularly the month of October, was formerly the time to begin again the laborious task of handfeeding many of the animals. It was the time for putting 'the fatting beasts to cabbage, carrots and turnips; dry cows to chaff; and the teams to chaff hay, mixed fodder or other dry food'. The teams were, of course, the oxen still used extensively on British farms a century and a half ago. Writing at the very beginning of the nineteenth century one authority suggested that with the commencement of autumn oxen should be supplied with 'an abundance of cut hay and straw, with an allowance of from 25 to 40 or 50 pounds weight of steamed turnips, cabbages or carrots per day, giving them, while at plough in autumn, such a proportion of oats and chaff as the size of the animal may require'.

All in all, livestock feeding has evolved considerably since that time and the job is now much simpler and more scientific. I well remember how quite recently winter feeding included the daily task of slicing mangolds for cattle, roots which had been hand-pulled on the previous day and loaded into a cart whatever the weather. October still sees the start of winter feeding but the work involved is generally much less muscular, and a balanced livestock diet is more assured.

Late autumn, the month of November in particular, saw the arrival of the moss-gatherers in damp, deciduous woods on both flanks of the Peak District. Even into recent times we occasionally came across their piled plastic bags under the trees, left to be filled on a return visit. They were a sort of gypsy people who came to the woods to collect the various mosses once common on trunks and gritstone boulders. The moss was bagged and sold to market gardeners and florists for wreath-making and for adding to composts. The moss-gatherers ripped the thick green moss-mat from the trees and stones and stuffed their bags. Another favourite place for the gatherers was the bed of the fast-flowing river but it was to the silent autumn wood that they came first, doing their work quickly and quietly. Public opinion would not be on their side nowadays because there has been a drastic decline in the number of species of moss in most parts of England. Atmospheric pollution is said to have caused it but the moss-gatherers cannot have helped matters.

The decaying foliage of oak, chestnut and birch produces what we romantically call the glory of the autumn woods, but more than these it is the beech – 'the Mother of Forests' – which catches the red rays of a setting sun and seems to turn into a blazing fire. If you are lucky enough to be crossing Haggwater Bridge or going up the old bridleway near Haggtor Coppice in the Woodlands Valley at such a time, you will see this sort of effect, highlight of the arboreal year. Of all south Pennine trees, though, it is the rowan or mountain ash which thrives in the least hospitable conditions, at the highest altitudes. It is, like all Britain's native fruit trees except the hazel, a member of the rose family; its berries are actually small apples and prized by birds like the mistle-thrush. The name rowan comes from the Old Norse *runa*, a charm. Quite late into the last century a branch of rowan was attached to the wall of cowsheds in this part of the country to ward off the attentions of hobgoblins and witches.

Up in the high country the rowan does not have much chance to show off in autumn. No sooner have its leaves turned golden brown than they are torn up by the October gales and whisked away across the steep clough-sides and out over the open moor.

Dark and Light and Silage Scent

The close of the year and the beginning of another – that is winter. The fingers of the clock which represents that year draw to and pass beyond twelve. This season brings its own delights of invigorating chill and sparkling skies and rushing streams and snow-crested heights. Winter is not the ogre it is often made out to be: it is as lovely as the rest.

Three particular qualities belong to winter: darkness, light and silence.

It must be hard for the town-dweller, particularly the young town-dweller, to realize the true significance of darkness. It is nowadays difficult to experience true and total darkness in our land but here and there, now and then, we may recall the true darkness of winter known long ago, before towns were so extensive and so well illuminated at night. In most parts of Peakland it is indeed difficult to find a really black night environment; even on the wilder moorland tops the orange glow of Manchester, Macclesfield and Sheffield diffuses into the sky and kills the illusion of wilderness.

I have noticed that the land is particularly well lit by man's distant invasion at times of thick cloud-cover, for then, of course, the glow is reflected all the more.

The countryman of long ago – even as recently as the war years – knew a virtually total blackness as he crossed the fields from farm to farm. Then, on nights without a moon, he really needed a stick to 'feel' the way and to give a third leg for better balance on steep or sticky going.

   Sometimes I find that utter blackness still, particularly in the wooded valleys near home. When there is no moon and the atmosphere is far from clear, I experience the thrill of unknown country, for the familiar terrain is quite unseen. In conditions of sharp frost the constant light of stars lights the way far more than is generally acknowledged. Venus, the brightest planet, can cause shadows on the frozen furrows.

   Long ago the lights of home were really a welcome sight for they were an oasis in the all-enveloping blackness of the winter night. None was greater master at the art of all descriptions of interior warmth than the Northamptonshire labourer John Clare. In his 'January – a Cottage Evening' the cosiness and safety of the labourer's parlour are done to perfection:

> Thus dames the winter night regales
> Wi wonders never ceasing tales.

The children twining between father's knees listen to the stories of things gone by and

> Quake wi the ague chills of fear
> And tremble while they love to hear
> Startling while they the tales recall
> At their own shadows on the wall.

Later they 'cringe away to bed' and scarce dare to 'look behind or make a noise'. They try to go to sleep and keep out fancy's fear but the wraiths persist –

> Witches on sheep trays gallop bye
> and faireys like to rising sparks
> Swarm twittering round them in the dark.

Sleep at last replaces fear, and the dark and silence of the winter night take over.

   Those winters Clare knew a century and a half ago were often keenly cold. His verse reflects careful observation and firsthand knowledge of the winter countryside. His 'January – a Winter's Day' is the first chapter of *The Shepherd's Calendar*, and in this month he enumerates the work and the pleasures of the heart of winter. His farm lad finds plenty to occupy the few hours of daylight; amongst the tasks is breaking the ice on the pond for the geese to swim and drink – the pond 'Which every night leaves frozen o'er then, when the hole is made, the birds "din his ears wi pleasures cry" and splash about 'ere it be froze again'.

Falling snow, and recently fallen snow, make familiar places all the more beautiful. Scenes usually treated with contempt by the eye take on arresting characteristics. Briefly, the fallen snow gives the present a glimpse of the rustic past.

The second quality of winter is light. When the clouds part after snowfall, when the blizzard has blown away to leave a pristine land, the sunlight shines with a radiant light. The dazzling light of heaven is reflected upwards to the sky as it is never reflected on any other occasion. The sparkling drifts curl their tops, and the light picks out their contours, blue and white and shades between. Then there is never a uniformity for the shading is etched across the landscape, and the cold clouds crossing the sky periodically break up that high wash of blue.

There is another light in winter, the light of the moon shining through the sharp, night air. The full moon of January can give unrealistic brilliance when an anticyclone rests steadily over Britain. I remember a week of moonlit walks in January 1973, when the diffused light of the moon through thin veils of fog illuminated the valley by the reservoirs. There were no recognizable shapes, only brightness all around. I emerged through a black line of trees and then up into the moon, and all was crystal clear across the white and frosty fields.

Up the hill towards the moon. Chesterfield's presence in the east was quite hidden by the low-lying fog, and for that I was grateful. Crossing those frosted fields I was reminded how such places seem greatly expansive – like prairies – in moonlight. Large fields seem to go on forever, and the monochrome everywhere gives a dream-world effect, a feeling of being lost in surroundings well known in daylight.

From the crest of the ridge by Pratthall two sounds brought me close to the world of the wild: a dog fox uttered its call from a distant wood near Priestfield Farm, and a tawny owl called from the fields above Cutthorpe. The owl's cry is always a homely sound, characteristic of understanding.

The uniformity of tones, of dark and light shades, in the winter's night makes a fascinating study. It can cast a spell so that the observer loses his bearings of time and place. In the most familiar woodland corners I have felt myself temporarily lost under a bright, winter moon. That stick is useful as an aid to

Deer in the snow at Chatsworth

balance in darkness, for it is surprising how easy it is to lose one's sense of the vertical and horizontal in the transition from a moonlit glade to the dark shadows beyond; at such a time a stick acts as an extra feeler or a prop. As with a blind man, so with a night wanderer, it can transmit changes of slope ahead when they are not visible. Likewise, a stick swung ahead in doubtful places proves the presence or absence of barbed wire.

The third quality of winter is silence. This can be experienced only infrequently in our crowded land. I have known utter silence in the early morning when crossing Kinder Scout in deep snow, between the head of Golden Clough and Seal Edge *en route* for the remote cabin in Oyster Clough upon Bleaklow. The eastern sky was broken by streaks of pink and yellow as I crunched through the knee-deep drifts, and here and there leapt the groughs.When I stopped and the crunching stopped, there was no sound for a time beneath that grey January sky so many years ago – then a grouse crossed low above the drifts, calling as it went.

There is also the silence of dank days, when fog creeps about the woods and no birds sing. That is the silence of death and best forgotten, as it so easily is when the skies clear and the low sun slants across the top of the birch woods. The mauve sheen of a birch wood when seen distantly is not quickly forgotten: it is one of the treasures of winter. Imperceptibly the mauve becomes silver, then green as the buds swell again with life, and winter fades over the hill.

The combination of fog and darkness is quite another thing. I was once told by an old villager the story of his homeward journey from the brickyard where he worked, over fields very familiar to him. So thick was the fog in the failing daylight that he became completely lost in a ten-acre pasture. Unable to find a wall, gate or stile, he wandered round until the fog cleared and the moon lit his way. Then there was the tractor driver who had to abandon his tractor because he could not find the gate into the lane leading to the farm. The retired postman once told me that he spent eighteen hours delivering letters on his usual round in the valley one fog-bound winter's day, a round he normally completed in three or four hours. A farmer spent half of the same murky night retrieving point-of-lay pullets from numerous tree-tops where they sought refuge after giving up the search for their cote. Fortunately he found all the birds, with the help of a ladder, a torch and a sack.

Occasionally we in the high country get the cobwebs blown away by a winter gale. Take, for instance, the great storm of 15–16

February 1962, when whole woods were torn up and rows of cottages and cowsheds and caravans lost their roofs.

'It was like a battlefield next morning,' one old lady remembered. 'I'd been waiting for the sweep for weeks but after that gale I didn't need him – the room was full of soot!'

A nearby poultry farmer lost three large henhouses, lifted bodily in the tempest and deposited virtually undamaged in another field. And no hens injured either. When he found the houses on their sides next morning, the hens were getting used to walking on one of the walls, and some had actually laid in the ventilators on the roof ridge. The shock, however, sent most of the birds into a moult later.

A job for January days on many farms long ago was the burning of lime to render it more useful as both a soil-neutralizer and a fertilizer. A manual of 1808 advised that, 'It is most advisable to burn it in a kiln; which is effected by depositing therein alternate strata of turf or coals and limestone, and the kiln being carefully closed, the process of calcination will be completed in about four hours.' Larger farms had such a kiln in or near the yard, though later it became more efficient to purchase lime already burnt at a quarry. Earlier in our own century local farmers would be seen setting out in the early morning with a cart and horses for the limestone quarries at Stoney Middleton or Peak Dale or Hillhead, returning at sunset with their heavy load. Next day, weather permitting, the burnt lime would be spread from the cart on to pastures and stubble fields. Lime-spreading by four-wheel-drive lorries working under contract has made this winter task much easier.

The place of the pig on the mixed farm has seen a revolution, too. It used to be usual for most farms to keep at least one pig for winter slaughter. I recall being told by an upland farmer some years ago how an old man he knew perhaps seventy years ago earned his living during the winter months by going round from farm to farm to kill the winter pig. On the killing day the farmer's wife got the copper on the boil early. After the dead pig had been bled, the 'pig-sticker' scraped the hairs from its skin while the helpers poured buckets of boiling water over the carcass to soften the skin. Later he would cut up the body into the appropriate portions. On the next day, the old farmer recalled, the family would rub salt and pepper into the meat, putting plenty on the 'skin side' and around the joints to dry up the meat. This task was usually carried out on a stone slab in the cellar, called a salting bank.

Another thing almost forgotten on our upland farms is the part played by herbs in winter keep. Ribgrass, for instance, used to be included in seed mixtures for hill sheep because it was a highly relished grazing plant. The wise shepherd realized that, 'A good taste means a contented belly.' Nettles may be considered pesky weeds nowadays and sprayed with herbicides along the stackyard edge and headland but they were once added to haystacks in thin layers between the thicker layers of hay as the stack was constructed. Nettles are rich in lime, potash and phosphoric acid. Their beneficial effect was well known by Welsh hill folk several centuries ago for it has always been their practice to dry and preserve nettles for making nettle 'tea' and 'beer' in the lean winter months for the supply of essential minerals when fresh vegetables were unobtainable.

Herbs play a less important part in the food supply of modern farm animals; they get their essential elements from such things as mangold and swede tops, which compare favourably with herbs in mineral content. Dried grass is one modern way of preserving the summer 'green' of a pasture, providing there are useful herbs in the crop. Drying, though, is now too costly, and silage-making is the great favourite, alongside traditional hay-making.

All over the Peak District we see evidence of silage-making and storage in half-ton bales wrapped in plastic bags. I used to think these shiny black bags a foul colour and wished manufacturers would use more natural colours. Now green bags are common, unfortunately there are several shades of green available. One of these is a shocking, quite unnatural green far more offensive to the eye than the standard black. Dull green or murky brown would be better colourings, blending with farmyards and hillside pastures reasonably well. Manufacturers take note!

And farmers take note! Many of their number have reason to mend their ways with the used plastic silage bags which so often lie abandoned where they were removed for feeding – to blow across the fields or hang offensively from trees where they became ensnared.

Winter is the season of the best farm aromas. As you walk through many villages or cross the fields near isolated farms, the lovely, heady scent of well-made silage drifts across. Years ago a common smell of similar type came from brewers' grains, particularly in the southern part of the Peak District where farms were close enough to Midland breweries to make the use of grains viable. We see and smell them less these days but good silage is just as good to the discerning nostrils. Following it in close second place is winter farmyard manure, the good stuff of the winter cowshed mixed with straw. Coming down through steep pastures above Chapel-en-le-Frith or close by Wincle, nothing complements the landscape of frosty hills and long shadows better than the savoury dairy farm aroma.

The good silage smell was in the air on a winter's morning as we climbed to Upper Elkstone above the Warslow Brook. Snow had drifted in the biting east wind that had blown for a week or more so that, as we turned along the farm drive that leads to a hill path to Black Brook, we had to cut our way over the shiny wave-crests of snow. No one had got to the first farm that way for some days – or weeks – and when we gained the yard we found it solid with piled snow-ice. Farmer Tunnicliffe's chimney was smoking, his Range Rover was caught in a line of drifts and his sheep clamoured near the outbuildings for hay put out in racks.

We stepped on towards Onecote, making easy progress on the drifts that bridged hawthorn hedges and stone walls. On that day of fierce frost under a duck-egg blue sky unsullied by even a single cloud our only companions were hungry, cackling magpies and dunnocks fluffed up against the elements to look twice their normal size. Silage was often in our nostrils through that shining day as we went by Onecote and Waterfall. All the hills were white, encased in a rock-hard mantle punctuated by black tree clumps. A solitary hare trotted over the snowed-over fields; a typical S. R. Badmin landscape.

As we crossed Grindon Moor, the bold grey bastion of Thor's Cave cliff poked above the chasm of the Manifold Valley. We could look down into this suggestion of a great rift, past Ladyside Farm to where the blue shadows of the interlocking spurs hemmed in the valley. Soon the huge white canvas of broad hills beyond the Manifold, towards Alstonefield and Hartington Nether Quarter, turned pink as the sun went down behind us. For a few moments the hill-tops ran with blood, then, quite suddenly, they were washed out and turned back through coral to palest blue. The day-long frost now took an even firmer grip as we made for Butterton's spire, slender sentinel on its snowy hilltop west of the Manifold.

An altogether different winter experience is remembered of the day of low and dark clouds as we made up to the top of Derwent Dale and over by Swains Head through patches of tiresome, wet snow. Down Far Black Clough we came by the young Etherow to the site of Woodhead's long-gone, castellated station. A cold wind blew little cheer up Longdendale as we sheltered by a culvert

Manifold Valley

where peaty moor-water crashed towards the river. Now we kept out of the wind for an hour or more, striding north-eastwards through the abandoned three miles and sixty-six yards of the new Woodhead Tunnel. It was relatively warm and totally calm in our concrete tube under the soggy heather moor – Britain's biggest civil engineering undertaking was only used for a few years and now serves only a handful of trespassing ramblers taking shelter or a short-cut between the head of Longdendale and the Upper Don.

Sunlight and in Spring
The late Geoffrey Winthrop Young – mountaineer and poet – saw the year as a curving line alongside another converging, curving line (Next Year). In his poetry he always travelled up the first curving line and looked down upon it from high above. Snow-capped Norway spruces stood at each end of the lines (where they met), and patchy snow and mud crossed the winter section. Greenness (presumably grass) crossed by a blue stream indicated summertime.

My own image of the year is quite clearly a clock-face, around which we pass in a clockwise direction. New Year is at one o'clock and midsummer at six. Here and there the expected colours intrude upon the face – white and black at two o'clock, green at five and six, yellow at eight and the brown smudge at ten merges with the white and black of midwinter. That is a half-dream, half-reality image held in the back of the mind for brief reference when the subject of the Year comes into consciousness.

That part of the year from three o'clock to five – greenish – is well summed up as 'sunlight, and in spring; and little else matters'. With Hardy of the south country I like the springtime, but perhaps for different reasons. Spring is truly 'the weather the cuckoo likes', and for me the lengthening days spell the freedom of wild places. Although we may stray into the dark woods and valleys upon a winter's night, there are restrictions to the delight at that season. Spring brings to my nostrils the post-teatime smell of fires:

> When the evening sunlight lingers
> And the blackbird's call
> Echoes across the garden, while, over the wall,
> The crackle of burning twigs.

Wallflower scent grows strong at sundown and children play among the mild shadows to

> Bring back golden memory
> Of childhood days in springtime.

The early days of spring have a remarkable propensity to be fickle. Suddenly a day in April can become still, cold and cloudy, with the countenance of winter. I remember such a day near the head of the lovely Moss Valley. We crossed the fields from Troway and down by the old dams above Ford. The leafless sycamores stood in black outline against the mirror surface of the dams whose water had once turned the several wheels to power machinery in the scythe and sickle works of this long-quiet dale. Nowadays the Moss and its tributary streams run down through rare-trod woodland and rolling acres below Sicklebrook, Povey and Plumbley. For all the advancing days of spring, that dull April weather in the Moss could have quite as well been November.

Most of true spring, though, has an intensity not easily mistaken. Of all the features of this season birdsong is the most noticeable – loud and constant birdsong throughout the daylight hours. Even after sundown the lapwings dance and call on the high, wet pastures. The dust behind the seed drill rises towards the lark poised on high and drifts away and is lost, like the short days of the dying season. We soon forget what has gone before and, if we are wise, thrill to the new-born season. That is the way to enjoy the turning year.

I remember a March day when we were passing along the western banks of the Emperor Lake at Chatsworth. Spring was certainly in the air, to judge by the great clamour arising from the far shore. It was a raucous conversation of the assembled ducks. A female mallard sailed by, framed by Scots pine branches and nearer hazel catkins which sent down puffs of bright pollen. The natural world has come to vibrant life around us.

Then again, spring can pull a surprise out of the bag for our delight: a sudden morning of unexpected brightness on waking; an overnight fall of snow which turns the world into different loveliness for a few, quiet hours before the rising sun disperses it, almost as quickly as it came. At such a time it is easy to wonder if the early morning snow-world was but a dream, for no sign of it remains by sundown.

The great ruin of the Empire Hotel at Buxton looked at its most forlorn before the buds burst on the surrounding deciduous trees. Though built about 1906 by the architect Thomas Garner, the Empire always seemed to me a thousand years old. It was a huge block in the Dutch style, long ago vacated and now taking on a special air of the mysterious when the spring zephyrs blew through distant corridors piled with fallen plaster, or when a door blew to in some upstairs room, or a window flapped and caught the sunlight. The large colony of jackdaws that inhabited the forest of chimneystacks added their calls to the enigma. Now the Empire and its aura have gone, though the springtime vision of it remains in photographs and in the memory.

The high plateaux of Peakland take on an extra magic with the lengthening days. At Nether Booth in the Edale Valley one can look up behind Lady Booth Farm to the brightening colours upon Edale Moor, eastern flank of Kinder Scout. The Shirt family has lived here at Lady Booth Farm for a long time, remembered as breeders of White-faced Woodland sheep, ancient breed of the gritstone uplands. Above Lady Booth it is but a short step across Nether Moor to the deep trough of Jaggers Clough with its broad bracken banks and scattered hawthorns which deck the valley with brilliant blossom when the cuckoo comes.

A 'jagger' was a man who looked after the 'jagging' horses which hauled loads of cleaned and dressed lead ore from mine to smeltmill. Such a name probably has its origins in a combination of the Old English word *cloh* (a cliff or steep place) and the old Norse word *gata* (a way or path) – hence 'a path across steep ground'. A jagger was, then, a man crossing such steep ground, and his loads became 'jags' – a term still quite common in the Peak District countryside.

From the headwaters of Jaggers Clough near the summit of Edale Moor it is only two miles to the top of Alport Castles, dominating Alport Dale as Britain's largest landslip. A quick descent into the Woodlands Valley, across the River Ashop and up the floor of Alport Dale soon brings one to the foot of this tower of detached gritstone. From the top of the tower there is a fantastic plateau vista across Bleaklow in clear weather. In the early part of the year the grass and heather tableland comes alive with brighter colour, and the calls of dunlins mingle with the familiar call of the curlew.

In gentler countryside dashes of sunlight illumine woods and vales. The increased intensity of the light improves quite remarkably the clarity of views at this period of the year. From the head of the Linacre Valley, west of Chesterfield, for instance, one can pick out clearly in bright, springtime weather details upon the magnesian limestone escarpment in the east which are not well seen in clear autumn and winter conditions. Barlborough Hall, the Oxcroft Settlement, Bolsover Castle and Hardwick Hall stand out more sharply than before.

Farm livestock are of particular interest in the context of this season. It is at this period that the placid Shire mare foals, and up and down the country she may still be discovered suckling her long-legged colt or filly. Lambs come straight to mind, of course, as part of the story of spring. Advances in the science of breeding have wrought a revolution in recent years, and more ewes are now lambing at times other than spring. Nevertheless, most lambs are still seen in the months from February to May.

Before me as I write is a small sepia photograph of two orphan lambs by a field gate well known to me. I found the old photograph in the empty farmhouse after the death of the last member of the old family. Those orphaned lambs probably grew up and raised their own lambs and have been dead these fifty years. 'Sunlight, and in spring; and little else matters' is truly the song of the season. Happiness with the freshness of the re-awakening world of nature, little thought of what may follow.

That valuable peck of March dust, which is, to the farmer, worth a king's ransom so that he can drill his spring crops, was just as valuable a century and more ago. At that time, though, some of his favourite crops would be comparative strangers to us. Tares, white beet, peas and potatoes would not cause us to raise our eyebrows; parsnips were looked upon as a worthwhile field crop as they appeared 'to be superior to almost any other root for fattening oxen, and especially swine'; chicory was widely used for grazing cattle and sheep and for making into hay. Furze – the miniature gorse – was, believe it or not, sown in March; in October the following year the crop was mown, bruised in a mill to destroy the sharp prickles and fed to cattle and horses. It was said that horses preferred recently bruised furze to hay, even corn, but I wonder how much feeding value it really had. Furze continued to grow for several years, producing from ten to fifteen tons per acre, and was stacked for winter use. Until well into this century there were a few crabmills left, the places where the furze was crushed.

A nuisance on farms at furze-feeding time (which still some-times occurs) was the heifer which persisted in sucking the udders of her companions. An animal well known to me – a polled Ayrshire/Shorthorn cross – developed this vice. Almost every night she managed to get loose by slipping the chain over her head (a thing she never did when she had horns), and then she proceeded to suck her neighbour almost dry. This done she often moved down the cowshed and drained two or three more cows before morning. Besides the loss of seven or eight gallons of milk per escapade, this nuisance soon caused her foster-mothers to dry up, because she left some milk in their udders. The only alterna-tives seemed to be to sell her or fasten her up in a shed with dry cows.

An old farm directory called 'a cowe which starteth to sucke those about her' nothing less than 'an evil thinge' and went on to suggest the use of 'bitter herbes mixed with vinegar and spread on the teates of the afflicted to stop her wasteful intentions'. No one, it seems, thought this worth trying, so she was packed off down the lane in the cattle waggon to market, so someone else inherited that particular bovine nuisance.

Another animal of that same herd went off to market because she had misbehaved herself one April day. Curiosity killed the cat, and curiosity is one of the traits of domestic cattle, too. One of the elder matrons of the herd was always investigating the unfamiliar. Once she noticed a bucket of eggs left in the yard and, sure enough, on withdrawing her nose she caught the rim and overturned the lot. Luckily only a few eggs were broken but it was typical that she, of the entire herd, should have seen (and reached) the egg bucket first. She was greedy too, and this proved her downfall. A barrowload of old barley swept from the barn floor was tipped under an overhanging hedge so that the hens could scratch it over. Within two hours the greedy cow had discovered the mouldy heap and, kneeling down, stretched under the hedge and with some difficulty consumed most of it. The result was that she soon became ill and lost her calf. It was too long a wait for her to produce another calf so she was sold to the butcher.

Halfway up a lane above Cordwell Valley, on Peakland's eastern edge, stand three derelict farms. Two of them have been empty since before the last war and are now in an advanced state of collapse, while up the fields behind is the third farm, empty these thirty-three years and showing signs of complete collapse. Talking to an elderly farmer not so long ago, I was told that in these three empty farms over a score of people lived sixty years ago. He recalled that in each case the man of the house was fond of drink, despite a meagre income.

'There's been some ale carted up that hill,' said my informant.

'How did they carry it up there?' I asked.

'Why!' he exclaimed. 'In their great, pot bellies, of course!'

If you wander there now on a spring day, the sprouting nettles are hiding the tumbled stones and fallen beams. The little wooden ladder used by fowls to gain their loft lies rotting on the ground; the deep well is filled in with rubble, and saplings block the doorway of the house on the knoll. Across the sloping pasture is a tiny, stone-walled enclosure where rhubarb and mint still flourish despite more than three decades of neglect.

On a bright April evening the larks still call over the pastures, and towering cumulus clouds can be seen standing in ranges above the far, eastern horizon. The happy calls of local children have not been heard here these seventy years; some of them are old folk now at the far corners of the earth, others live in nearby villages and remember with affection their hard and happy upbringing at Bank Green.

Across the other side of the Peak District I spent a memorable day on the brown moorlands above the Tame Valley. April was giving way to May, and waders had returned to the high ground – dunlins were piping across Wimberry Moss and a pair of agitated curlews came calling in the breeze, unhappy that we were crossing their breeding territory.

If spring is the time when the moor-birds are at their most

Alsop-en-le-Dale

active, it is also the season of some of our loveliest skies: April of the brown-shaded clouds, piled and broken shapes with shafts and slanting sunbeams between. Even views across the flat sweeps of still-brown spring moorland, as across Wimberry Moss to Windgate Edge, are rendered dramatic by those fine cloudscapes amid the open sweep of sky. Down on the moor's face there is the grey flash of a mountain hare, still in winter overcoat, zipping away on the bilberry tussocks. A closer look reveals the humble lemon blooms of the hare's tail making a brave showing above the tired, oozing heaths. Its conspicuous cousin, common cotton grass, will take over later in summer to brighten broad expanses of the same moorlands.

Miles to the south the vistas out to the west from the Lyme estate's Park Moor are lusher, greener, altogether prettier and less dramatic. Piled-up cumulus clouds fill the Cheshire sky over the plain, and close at hand we look past ewes and lambs and budding rhododendrons to upstanding Scots pines making an almost Oriental frieze. And always those white ice-towers of cauliflower clouds and a blue-grey dash of some half-imagined hail squall out over the rich pastures beyond Prestbury and

Alderley Edge. We're on the edge of Tunnicliffe's own country, described in an earlier chapter. These views of the plain from the western hills of the Peak District are those which appear in some of his best-known etchings of the twenties – *The Forest of Macclesfield*, with the chimneys of Macclesfield and the plain beyond, *The Bull* doing battle with a tree root, the tree-lined plain behind, and *The Cheshire Plain* with three cattle at the edge of a hill and the huge space of hedgerows and trees looking west beneath a watery sky, probably his most famous etching.

From the photographer's point of view, spring is often a much better time of year than summer: skies cleared by showers, often filled by interesting cloud structures, and trees still bare and more architectural than in dark, laden days of high summer. So often is photography – both monochrome and colour – more rewarding before the sun reaches its zenith on Midsummer's Day. Spring, though, is a comparatively short time of year. The evenings have barely started to get light than the first cuckoo call is heard, the swallows are dipping in a hundred farmyards, and the season is ended.

The Picnic Party and the Bluebell Wood

A recurring vision of summer is, for me, a woodland glade, deep shadowed and far from any pathway. Bright leaves of birch and beech and oak hang still in the heady sunshine cast down by flashing birch trunks. It is always summertime in that glimpse of paradise, a well-loved woodland world where the magic of the years lives on.

At the edge of the wood, a stout middle-aged lady sits with wide-brimmed straw hat, a sash of red about it, and arranges a picnic on a white cloth spread upon the sward. About her the family come and go – one with water from a crystal spring, another with bracken fronds to fan away the flies, and others play out in the hot pasture. Memory and imagination mingle to form a canvas painted with rich colours; the woodland and the people associated with it. The woodland remains but its associations are but memories, always illuminated with a summer sun.

A feature of that woodland – above any other known to me – is the profusion of bluebells which glorify its floor in earliest summer. No photograph or painting can do full justice to woodland when such a blue carpet is spread by way of welcome to this high point of nature's year.

Few men toil now from sunrise to sunset in the open air. Theirs was a thirst of the gods. John Clare, of course, knew the honourable thirst of the summer – the sweating scythesman who finds a growing sorrel,

> Called 'sour grass' by the knowing clown
> The mower gladly chews it down
> And slakes his thirst the best he may
> When singing brooks are far away.

Throughout summertime in his masterpiece *The Shepherd's Calendar* (1824) the theme of thirst recurs, alongside references to the visitations of insects in the open air – his mention of gadflys and horse bee and pismires (ants) reminds the reader that, though July was the month 'when everywhere's a vale of dew' and

> Daughter of pastoral smells and sights
> And sultry days and dewy nights,

there were snags in the rural paradise of a century and a half ago. They were small snags, though, and summer was happy and full of worthwhile activity.

The shepherd finds early summer a busy time. In John Clare's days all flocks were washed in stream or river-bend, to clean the wool before shearing. The sheep were taken

> To wash pits where the willow shadows lean
> Dashing them in their fold stained coats to clean.

Here and there throughout the gritstone country we can still see the neglected sheepfolds where the hill flocks were gathered for inspection and for dipping in the adjacent stream. Look, for instance, round secret corners of the Westend or Upper Derwent and you will see the tumbled, drystone enclosures where the flocks were dashed into the crystal current on long-gone summer days.

The lambs are growing large by mid-summer, and orphan lambs become less dependent on the suckling bottle. They still follow their foster parent about though and show no fear of the shepherd's dogs. Orphaned lambs, given the chance, will stay close to man all their lives.

Cool shadows of a summer wood are the more welcome after the heat of open fields. When the bluebells have faded and bent their heads, the foxglove stirs in clearings and headlands –

> Dark beneath the beech
> In summer comes the shade.

Coming now to water, the heady scent of meadowsweet (the wild spiraea) is still, fortunately, a common plant. It raises its pale yellow flowers as clusters of lemon foam on stems a yard high in boggy places and stream margins. Of all the water-loving plants of the summer months, my favourite is the early blooming kingcup; the marsh marigold comes early in summer (really a spring and summer flower) and lights up wet places with its splash of butter. The loveliest kingcups known to me beautify the shallow upper reaches of a Derbyshire reservoir where the families of frogs create a continuous rippling and sallow over-hangs the steady surface not far away. An occasional trout meanders beneath the gold reflections seeking lazily a wandering afternoon gnat.

Summer skies can often be remarkable for their brilliance and variety. On a crystal morning great promise radiates from the sky, when no cloud is to be seen and the day seems poised for great events. Later small islands of fracto-cumulus mark the passage of the hottest hours, small fair weather wool-packs sailing slowly upon a peaceful sky. Such clear, summery weather often follows a period of damper conditions and heavier cloud. The returning brightness is then all the more welcome, and the clarity of sky and landscape impresses upon the observant viewer the potential beauties of the land about.

Thunderstorms were once dreaded phenomena. Viewed logi-cally, they are a magnificent natural spectacle and add the edge of variety to the summer hills and vales. The greatest storms of my experience have taken place in high mountain country, though many fine ones come to mind in the context of Peakland. Huge towers of cumulus, cauliflower heads of purest white and pink and yellow, lift across the moorland heights and across the coal-measure country of the east when conditions are ideal for storm-generation.

All one hot afternoon the air above Cordwell grew ever thicker. Grey-brown vapours filled the sky above Rose Wood and Moorhall. We had finished milking when the first lightning flickered far over lonely Meanfield Farm. Dull rumblings came soon after, and on my homeward race against the hail-sheets lacing the western sky those rumblings drew nearer. Atop the grim pall were white-edged woolpacks, their crests broken by straight lines of frozen vapour where the hailstones were forming upon high. Such intermissions between the warning and the onset of nature's fury are intensely thrilling times, as when the first snowflakes herald wonderful blizzards.

When the rain-sheets have passed and the sun returns, the land reappears with greater brilliance. In summer the brilliance evolves through the maturing season; the changing colourscape is one of nature's jewels which precludes any chance of boredom, of sameness. From a favourite ridge-top belvedere I watch the passage of the season. The far fields beneath the conspicuous wood (all of 4½ miles distant) are a quilt of brown and green as spring fades. Soon thereafter all is the vivid green of lively pasture, accumulating mow meadow and leaping corn. In high summer the mow meadows turn beige and dun as the grasses flower and are cut down and the made hay is carted away. Green pasture, brown meadow and green corn. As the evenings shorten and the cuckoo's call is but a memory, the cornlands flash gold between the darkening green of wood and pasture and restored meadow. All along the distant ridge from my perch one can see the fruitful corn on a sunny day; it is a wonderful sight when little clouds float across and cast their momentary shade – first upon green, then upon gold.

Now, though, I see in my mind's eye a pre-war party of ramblers. They are sitting on a breezy summer hill-top, somewhere in Peakland, with a bright sky behind them; they are laughing and chatting, clothed in typical outdoor wear of the period. There are young women in tweed skirts and ankle socks and tough nailed boots, men with open-necked shirts and shorts, and older men in baggy plusfours. It is a summer Sunday outing of the Sheffield Clarion Ramblers resting high in the gritstone country. I imagine Bert Ward, of course, presiding over the day and telling the party about incidents from rambles in the high country long since passed.

G. H. B. Ward, 'the King of Ramblers' to his many friends and acquaintances in the pre-war outdoor movement, was born in June 1876, the son of a Sheffield mechanic, less than two miles from the city centre. His was a working-class background, and his mother died when he was only ten. However, his father was a real character (described in retrospect as a brilliant rarity) and brought up his son with love and imagination, leaving him no money but 'a fortune he could never spend – a love of the open air'. After leaving school Bert became an engineer at Messrs Hatfields' steelworks in the city, and a Sunday School teacher at St John's in the Park.

The ideals of Socialism appealed to him from an early date and he was much influenced by the thinking of the pioneer Socialist Edward Carpenter, who lived at Bradway and later at Millthorpe, south-west of Sheffield. Bert became the first Secretary of

Ramshaw Rocks from Morridge

the Labour Representation Society in the city. He taught himself Spanish and became an authority on Spain and its people. He wrote *The Truth about Spain*, which became a standard work on that country in the 1930s. He also wrote with authority about municipal milk supplies for a London borough.

When the Ministry of Labour was formed and people well known in Labour circles were recruited, Bert was one of them, spending much time in Whitehall during the 1914–18 war. After the war he served as Chief Officer at the Conciliation Department of the Ministry of Labour, covering the country between Berwick-upon-Tweed and Leicester. He occupied this onerous post until reaching retirement age in 1941. But that was but one side of his interests and life's work, and retirement brought no rest to this restless spirit.

Writing in 1958, James Dobby stated that G.H.B.'s father set the seed which was to germinate into his love of the countryside. 'For young Bert can be said to have been one of the first ramblers, if not the first,' Dobby wrote. His first activities were a week's walking in Lakeland and a long week-end in Dovedale, the latter reached on foot from Bakewell. In 1900 he married and in that year he founded the well-known – and still active – Sheffield Clarion Ramblers, which was claimed as the first active rambling club in Britain. The first organized walk took place on the first Sunday in September 1900, when the round of Kinder Scout was completed. On that historic day Bert led thirteen kindred spirits from Edale station, over Jacob's Ladder (then virtually un-trodden, not the 'broken ruin' it is today) and Edale Cross to Hayfield; then over by the head of Ashop Clough to the Snake Inn, where they caused a stir by asking for tea. Lacking sufficient bread, the landlord's family set to and baked some for the party. New cakes, boiled ham and tea cost them 1s.3d. each. They carried on by Hope Cross to Hope station and so ended the first organized Sunday ramble ever made.

In his appreciation of Ward, James Dobby explained that the club's founder was not content with 'just a club' – he had to have a way to publicize its rambles and aims, to share the knowledge that was his, attained by research and hard study, personal contact with members of families who had farmed in the moorland areas for centuries, and by bitter experience – so he published *The Sheffield Clarion Ramblers Handbook*. The first edition came out in 1910 and set the pattern for all subsequent issues, up to its demise over fifty years later. The first section of each handbook contained details of future rambles, including bus/tram/train times and fares, route, distance and leader's name. Then followed a miscel-lany of local stories, histories, literary pieces (including verse), maps, reports of meetings and photographs. Most of the contents came from Bert's own pen, and continued to do so up to his death. They are now collectors' items.

For years, he remembered later, he had to ask the men to realize that there were women who had legs too – and that they were capable of using them for long-distance walking. He invented a couple of slogans for use in the handbook; the first was 'A rambler made is a man improved', and this appeared as a sub-title on the front cover of each handbook. The other was, 'The man who never was lost never went very far.' Both slogans have been synonymous with their inventor ever since.

It is difficult for younger people to appreciate the restrictions imposed by landowners of the highest and most attractive ground right up to 1939. The National Trust owned only tiny pockets of land, and everywhere else had few public rights of way. The cockpit of trouble between jealous landowners and a growing army of ramblers was the Peak District. Secateurs and wire-cutters were carried by most early rambling leaders to help parties reach open moorland. Farmers were hostile to 'tres-passing' walkers on the lower slopes, and gamekeepers hated them on the moorlands above. James Dobby recalled that, 'Gamekeepers hated Bert Ward and so did their gaffers. He, in turn, had scant respect for most of the landowners.' He came in time to realize that one club – the Sheffield Clarion – could not tackle the problem alone with any hope of success, so in 1912 he formed the Hallamshire Footpaths Preservation Society, and in 1926 the Sheffield and District Federation of the Ramblers' Association, becoming Chairman of the latter until his death. He was elected a Fellow of the Royal Geographical Society in 1922.

In March 1926 the Sheffield Ramblers' Association united with that from Manchester for the famous demonstration rally in the Winnats Pass, near Castleton. By 1928 other federations had formed elsewhere, and Bert realized the need for a national body. This finally came into being as the National Standing Council of Ramblers' Federations (later called more conveniently the Ramblers' Association) in 1931, with Bert as Chairman and Stephen Morton as its first Secretary. Another outcome was the formation of the Peak District Branch of the Council for the Preservation (later Protection) of Rural England, so G.H.B. can fairly be called a founder of this important branch of the national body.

In 1938 the Access to the Mountains Act became law but no financial aid was allocated to any organization and a £2 fine (with the costs of both parties) was instituted for the act of trespass (without proof of damage to property) so that, in fact, the rambling movement gained nothing and lost something into the bargain with the passing of the Act.

In 1934 Bert revised John Derry's *Across the Derbyshire Moors*, something of a classic by a pioneer rambler, and again in 1939. He proved to be a fine researcher, as shown by many articles on Enclosure Acts, prehistoric remains, old rights of way and so on in the Clarion Handbooks. It must not be thought that all this work kept him at home. Throughout his life he walked great distances in wild country in all weathers. C. B. Harley once wrote that he had seen faster leaders but never anything so regular and relentless as Bert's long-legged stride over rough ground right into old age. Stephen Morton remembers him as a wiry, dark man of medium height who looked taller than he actually was. He had the eyes of a visionary and, though he had a speech impediment, was a great orator.

Typical of his enthusiasm was the occasion when Bert gave a lecture to ramblers at the Gambit Café, in Commercial Street, Sheffield. Everyone was told to bring along a map of the area, and the lecture began, the speaker conducting his audience in imagination across miles of interesting country. By 10.30 p.m. the waitresses became restless and made their displeasure obvious.

'We haven't finished yet,' said Bert. 'Have you a booking for tomorrow evening?'

'No,' came the reply.

'Right! You have now,' he said triumphantly, and the lecture continued the next evening!

His first concern was always for the welfare of the party in his charge on the hills. His map-reading and compass work were faultless. In those far-off days before World War II, the train was the normal means of transport – often the 6.35 a.m. from Sheffield's Victoria Station to Penistone or Woodhead or points farther west.

C. B. Harley recalls one occasion in the early 1930s when a morning of 'bog-walloping over the tops' brought the party to the head of the River Derwent in stormy conditions. They went on by Howden Edge and Crow Stones Edge to Margery Hill. They then continued southwards 'to meet half a gale of wind and rain'. In two miles they came to a broken wall, and Bert explained in detail the significance of Seward's Lode, a Saxon boundary ditch, before continuing 'a flattish mile of really vicious water-logged nigger-heads' to come down to Abbey Brook and Derwent Dale. The party was very tired, but 'Bert was striding out like a Martian'.

His physical prowess continued into old age. In April 1951 he took two journalists onto Big Moor, not far from his home (Storth Lodge, Moorwoods Lane, near Holmesfield, high on the hills to the south of Sheffield and in full view of the city). The party travelled by car; it was a very cold day. As usual Bert had no coat, scarf or gloves, and his waistcoat and jacket were undone and flapping in the strong wind. Snowflakes were going down the top of his breeches. After a long walk in the tempest Bert strode on ahead of the others (he was approaching his seventy-fifth birthday) and got back to the road first. Here he slowly sank to the ground. His dead weight could not be raised but with the help of a passing motorist he was pulled into a car and driven home. The doctor prescribed at least three days in bed to recover from exhaustion and exposure but a couple of evenings later Bert was delivering a lecture over the moors in Baslow – whether he had walked there from Storth Lodge is not recorded!

The ramblers of Sheffield bought the 54½ acres on the summit of Lose Hill and presented the deeds to G.H.B. in appreciation of his life's work. Two thousand ramblers joined him on the summit on a fine April day in 1945, when he was handed the deeds of what has ever afterwards been called 'Ward's Piece'. He was much moved by this gesture of thanks and claimed to have at last joined 'the gaffers' against whom he had waged war for so long to obtain public access to the hills. At the same ceremony Bert in turn presented the deeds to the National Trust. That was one of the highlights of a long life; another came near the end. He was lying in a Sheffield hospital in July 1957, unable to attend the annual degree congregation of Sheffield University to receive the honorary degree of Master of Arts, so a special extension was held in the hospital ward.

'Our tribute today cannot match the splendour of a windswept hilltop, but we hope that it gives a modest satisfaction,' said Professor Laughton.

G.H.B. died in October 1957, leaving sufficient material for several issues of the *Clarion Ramblers Handbook*. In the early 1960s this classic work ceased publication, though the Sheffield Clarion Ramblers Club is still very much alive. Whereas the majority of outstanding early ramblers walked out of necessity, Bert Ward did so out of a true passion for the activity; furthermore he was a man of vision – some would call it genius – and he unselfishly gave all his energies to the fostering of rambling, the maintenance of rights of way and the encouragement of the formation of bodies to protect the ordinary man's rights in the countryside. He was, in fact, a true pioneer of the modern concept of outdoor activities. The thousands of ramblers of all ages who now tramp the open moors and mountains of Britain have much to thank one Sheffield native for.

Our imagined pre-war Clarion party resting on that breezy summer hill-top knew the district before the popular paths were beaten tracks and cars snarled up the twisting lanes. Few of them owned cars. This business of car-ownership is a mixed blessing: for the dedicated hill wanderer a car gives access to country somewhat denied the rambler of old but nevertheless public transport was surprisingly comprehensive in those days. By

Rocking stones, Crow Stones Edge, Howden Moors

judicious use of bus and train, parties were able to arrange long days, starting and finishing in different places – impossible for the car-bound walker without complicated joint efforts. A glance at *Clarion Ramblers Handbooks* proves this.

On Sunday 4 August 1935 the party left Sheffield Midland Station on the 8.35 a.m. train, alighted at Grindleford and walked twenty miles via Baslow, Chatsworth Park and Bakewell to Ashford, Monsal Head, Eyam and back to Grindleford in time for the 8.8 p.m. train for Sheffield. Return fare 10d. On another day later that year they met at Middlewood tram terminus, in the north of the city, at 9.30 a.m. and walked by Oughtibridge, Bolsterstone and High Bradfield to Hollow Meadows and Fulwood – eighteen miles, tram fare 3d.

Keen ramblers like the late Vera Roper and her friends travelled far and wide on public transport and covered long

The western portal of Totley Tunnel at Padley, near Grindleford

distances in the southern Pennines and in mountains far away. On the other side of the Peak District at this time the Manchester Rucksack Club was thriving in the same way. Men like the late Fred Heardman, Donald Berwick and many more were covering great distances in parties large and small, running the gauntlet of opposition by protective landowners and their employees.

So it is that each summer finally declines. The first brown furrows are seen across the golden land as ploughs already prepare for next year's green and gold. The year slides imperceptibly out of summer as the clock approaches nine. Birdsong fails and the well-loved woodland world grows silent; no more is the flash of a red sash seen near the bluebell carpet, for the picnic party has gone home.

Bibliography

Mary Andrews, *Long Ago in Peakland* (Milward, 1955)

B. Bunker, *Cruck Buildings* (1970)

Roy Christian, *Derbyshire* (Batsford, 1978)

Brian Cooper, *Transformation of a Valley – the Derbyshire Derwent* (Heinemann, 1983)

J. B. Firth, *Highways and Byways in Derbyshire* (Macmillan, 1905)

(Ed.) Trevor Ford and J. H. Rieuwerts, *Lead Mining in the Peak District* (Peak Park Planning Board, 1968)

(Ed.) Trevor Ford, *Limestone and Caves of the Peak District* (Geo Books, 1977)

Jack Hanmer, *Walks around Glossop*

Thomas Middleton, *Legends of Longdendale*

R. Millward and A. Robinson, *The Peak District* (Eyre Methuen, 1975)

C. P. Nicholson and P. Barnes, *Railways in the Peak District* (Dalesman, 1971)

N. Pevsner, *The Buildings of England: Derbyshire* (Penguin, 1953)

Lindsey Porter, *The Peak District – Pictures from the Past* (Moorland, 1984)

W. A. Poucher, *The Peak and Pennines* (Constable, 1973)

———, *The Yorkshire Dales and the Peak District* (Constable, 1984)

Joyce Powell, *Longdendale in Retrospect*

Roger A. Redfern, *Rambles in Peakland* (Robert Hale, 1965)

———, *Portrait of the Pennines* (Robert Hale, 1969)

———, *Peakland Days* (Robert Hale, 1970)

———, *Walking in England* (Robert Hale, 1976)

———, *South Pennine Country* (Robert Hale, 1979)

Walt Unsworth, *Portrait of the River Derwent* (Robert Hale, 1971)

(Ed.) G. H. B. Ward, *Across the Derbyshire Moors* (Sheffield Newspapers)

Keith Warrender, *High Peak Faces and Places* (Willow, 1978)

———, *Exploring Longdendale* (Willow, 1980)

Index

Abbey Grange Cottage, 175
Abney, 32
Abney Low, 34
Abney Moor, 29
Agden Clough, 18
Agden Reservoir, 19
Agden Rocher, 18
Alphin Pike, 156
Alport Castles, 199
Alport Dale, 199
Alsop-en-le-Dale, 83, 84
Ashbourne, 91–3
Ashford-in-the-Water, 70
Ashop Farm, 39
Ashopton Viaduct, 39
Ashway Gap House, 155
Ashway Rocks, 154

Bagshaw, 144, 145
Bagshaw, William, 145, 146
Bailey Hill, Bradfield, 18
Bakewell, 93–5
Ballidon, 84
Bamford, 51, 52
Banktop Farm, Derwent Dale, 44
Bar Brook, 25
Barrel Inn, Bretton, 34
Beeston Tor, 122, 123
Bellhagg Farm, 164
Bents House, 16
Beresford Dale, 110
Bertram, St, 122
Berwick, Donald, 163, 215
Biggin-by-Hartington, 181
Biggin Dale, 182
Big Moor, 25, 210
Bill's o'Jack's Plantation, 154
Birchover, 74

Black Brook, 144
Black Hill, 157, 158
Black Moss, 158
Blore, 125, 126
Bole Hill Quarry, Padley, 49
Bollington, 141
Bollin, River, 133
Bolsterstone, 20
Boot, Charles, 16
Boot's Folly, 16
Bosley Minn, 132
Boulsover, Thomas, 62
Bowsen Barn, Bradfield, 18, 19
Bradbourne, 86
Bradbourne Brook, 83
Bradfield, 17, 18
Bradfield Dale, 15–20
Bradfield Low, 17
Brassington, 85
Bretton Clough, 29, 32–5
Bretton Clough Twin Farms, 32, 33
Bretton Village, 29, 33–5
Broadmeadow Hall, 113
Brook House, 167
Broomhead Hall, 21
Broomhead Moors, 21
Broomhead Moss, 158
Broomhill, 55
Butterton, 118
Buxton, 95–8

Callow Farm, Hathersage, 185
Canyard Hills, 20, 21
Carlecotes, 160–2
Carsington, 87, 88
Carsington Reservoir, 87
Castern Hall, 125
Castle Hill, Bradfield, 18

Castle Ring, 81
Cauldron Low, 124
Chapel-en-le-Frith, 98, 99
Charles Head, 143
Cheshire Gritstone Trail, 133
Chew Brook, 153–6
Chew Reservoir, 156
Chinley Churn, 144
Chrome Hill, 114
Cliffe House Farm, 19, 20, 55
Clod Hall, 25
Cockey Farm, Abney, 34
Colborne Hill, 54
Cordwell Valley, 25, 175, 201, 205
Cotton, Charles, 110
Cotton Famine Road, 158
Cowburn Tunnel, 54
Cratcliffe Tor, 76, 77, 80
Croker Hill, 133
Crowdecote, 113
Crowden Great Brook, 157
Curbar Gap, 25
Cut Gate, 45, 166, 167, 169

Dale Dike Reservoir, 16, 17
Dane, River, 129
Darley Dale, 73, 74
Dearden Clough, 159
Deer Hill, 159
Derbyshire and Lancashire Gliding
  Club, 35
Derwent Dale, 41, 44, 195
Derwent Edge, 15
Derwent Reservoir, 41, 44
Dick Hill, 153, 154
Don, River, 159
Don Valley, 19
Don Well, 159
Dore, 55–9
Dove Head, 115
Dovestone Edge, 155
Dovestone Reservoir, 156
Dove Valley, 109–15
Dowel Cave, 114
Dumkins, 132, 133
Dunford Bridge, 159, 160

Eastern Moors, 21, 24, 26, 27
Eccles Pike, 144
Ecton Hill, 118
Edale, 53, 54

Edale Head House, 163
Elderbush Cave, 122
Eldon Hill, 66, 69
Eldon Hole, 65–9
Elliott, Ebenezer, 38
Elmin Pitts Farm, 39, 40
Emley Moor, 45, 166
Emperor Lake, Chatsworth, 198
Empire Hotel, Buxton, 198
Ewden Valley, 20, 21
Eyam Moor, 29

Fairholmes, Derwent, 41
Flash, 127
Flash Head, 115
Flask Edge, 27
Flouch Inn, 45, 162, 166
Ford, 123
Ford Hall, 145, 146
Fox House, 59, 60
Furness, Richard, 57

Gawsworth, 137, 140
Giant's Hole, 70
Ginnett House, Ladybower, 40, 41
Glossop, 100, 101
Godfrey's Cross, 25
Goldsitch Moss, 127, 129
Gotheridge Farm, 32
Gradbach, 129
Grainfoot Farm, 40
Greenfield Brook, 154
Greenfield Paper Mill, 156
Grimbocar Wood, 39
Grindleford, 47
Grindon, 119

Haggwater Bridge, 187
Hall, Muriel, 61
Hallfield, 16, 174
Hamps, River, 123, 124
Harthill Moor, 76, 80
Hartington, 109, 112
Hathersage, 49–51
Havenhill Dale Brook, 85, 86
Hayfield, 148
Hazelford Hall, 29
Hazelhead, 162
Hazelton Clump, 126
Heardman, Fred, 163, 215
Heathcote Museum, Birchover, 77

Helliwell, Ivy, 174, 175
Henmore Brook, 83, 86, 87
Highlow Hall, 29, 32
Hingcliff Hill, 167
Hipley Dale, 85
Hognaston, 89
Hognaston Winn, 89
Holdworth, 19
Hollinsclough, 114
Holme Moss, 45, 157, 158, 159
Hope, 53
Hope Valley, 47
Hopton, 87–9
Hordron, 169, 170
Houndkirk Moor, 60
Howden Edge, 45
Howden Reservoir, 41
Hulme End, 116, 117
Hunter, J., 17
Hurst Clough, Hope Valley, 51

Ilam, 123, 125

Jacob's Ladder, 163
Jagger's Clough, 198, 199
Jarvis Clough, 38

Kerridge, 141
Kerridge Hill, 141, 142
Kettleshulme, 141, 143
Kinder Scout, 54, 192, 198
Kirk Edge Convent, 19
Kniveton, 89, 90

Ladybower Clough, 35, 38
Ladybower Reservoir, 35, 38–41
Lady Cross, 25
Langley, 135, 136
Langsett, 165
Laund Clough, 170
Leadmill Bridge, 29
Leash Fen, 26, 27
Leek, 101
Leek and Manifold Light Railway,
    116, 117
Little Don Valley, 20, 165
Loftshaw Clough, 170
Long Causeway, 61
Longdendale, 157, 159
Longnor, 115
Longshaw Lodge, 59, 60

Lose Hill, 211
Lower Elkstone, 118
Lyme Hall, 143, 202

Macclesfield, 101–3
Magpie Mine, Sheldon, 70, 71
Malcoff, 146
Manifold Valley, 115–26, 195
Marsden, 159
Matlock, 103, 104
Mayfield Valley, 61
Mickleden Clough, 166
Midhope Moors, 166
Midhopestones, 170, 171
Moorseats, Hathersage, 50
Moscar, 35
Mytham Bridge, 51, 52

Navio, Brough, 51
Nether Ashop Farm, 39
Nether Booth, 164
Nether Bretton Farm, 34
Nether Hurst, Hope Valley, 51, 52
Nether Shatton, 52, 53
Netherton, 86
New Mills, 148–51
Newton, William, 34
Nine Stones Circle, Harthill Moor, 80

Offerton Moor, 29, 184
Onecote, 123, 195
Onesmoor, 19
Oyster Clough, 192

Padley, 47, 48
Padley Chapel, 48, 49
Padley Mill, 47
Parkhouse Hill, 114
Parkin Clough, 35
Parwich, 84
Peak Forest Canal, 144
Penistone, 45, 104–6
Pennine Way, 157, 158
Pilsbury, 112, 113
Porter (Little Don) Valley, 165, 167,
    169, 171
Portway, the, 80, 81
Pott Shrigley, 142, 143
Priddock Wood, 38

Rainow, 141

Ramsden Clough, 159
Ramshaw Rocks, 127
Ramsley Moor, 24, 25
Reynard's Cave, Dovedale, 110
Ridgewalk Moor, 44
Riding House, Derwent, 40
Ringinglow, 60, 61
Roaches, the, 127
Robin Hood's Stride, 76, 77
Ronksley Farm, 41, 44
Roper, Vera, 214
Rowlee Farm, 164, 165
Rowsley, 72
Rowtor Rocks, 74–6
Rucksack Club, 215
Rushup Vale, 69, 70
Russet Well, Castleton, 68, 70

Saddleworth, 106, 107, 154
Saddleworth Moor, 154
Scarratt's Stone, 170
Sett, River, 146, 148–51
Sett Valley Trail, 148
Sheen, 116
Sheep sales, 180
Sheffield, 55
Sheffield Clarion Ramblers, 175, 206,
    208–15
Sheldon, 70
Shell Brook, 132
Shepherd's Meeting Stones, 45, 46
Shepherd Wheel, 61
Shillito Plantation, 25
Shrigley Hall, 142, 143
Shutlingsloe, 133
Slippery Stones, 45
South Head, 146
Stanage Pole, 61
Stanton-in-Peak, 70
Stanton Moor, 76, 77
Stanton Woodhouse, 73
Stocksbridge, 20
Strawberry Lee, Dore, 59
Strines, 15, 16
Sutton Common, 133, 136, 140
Sutton Lane Ends, 135, 136, 137
Swindon, 167, 168, 169

Tagg, Joseph, 41
Tame, River, 153

Thornhill, 53
Thor's Cave, 119, 122, 195
Throwley Hall, 125
Tilbury, Gervase of, 65
Torrs, the, 150
Totley Moor, 21, 22, 24, 27
Totley Tunnel, 47
Townhead, 160
Townsend, Joe, 39, 40
Tunnicliffe, Charles, 133–40, 203

Underbank Farm, 39
Upper Booth, Edale, 164
Upper Elkstone, 118, 123, 195
Upper Midhope, 171, 174
Upper Padley estate, 49

Ward, G. H. B., 25, 27, 33, 55, 61,
    163, 167, 169, 206–15
Ward's Piece, 211
Warslow, 117
Warslow Brook, 117, 118
Waterfall, 125
Weag's Bridge, 119
Wessenden Head, 158
Wessenden Valley, 158
Westend Valley, 44
Wetton, 122
Whaley Bridge, 144
Wharncliffe Side, 19, 20
Whinstone Lee Tor, 40
Whirlow Hall Farm, 59
White, Nancy, 141
Whiteley Wood, 62
Whitworth, Joseph, 74
Wildboarclough, 180
Wimberry Moss, 156, 201, 202
Wimberry Rocks, 156
Win Hill, 35, 38, 39
Wincle, 132
Wincle Grange, 132
Wincle Minn, 132, 133
Wirksworth, 107, 108
Withens Edge, 159
Woodhead, 159, 166, 195
Woodhead Tunnel, 159, 196
Woodlands Valley, 164, 187

Yorkshire Bridge, 35, 38, 39